SE ~~ASON OF~~
EM

Daily Reflections for Advent,
Christmas, and Epiphany

Kay Murdy

the columba press

Editorial director: Nick Wagner
Prepress manager: Elizabeth J. Asborno

First published in 1996 by

the columba press

55A Spruce Avenue
Stillorgan Industrial Park
Blackrock, Co Dublin

in association with

Resource Publications, Inc.
160 E. Virginia Street #290
San Jose, CA 95112-5876

Reprint Department
Resource Publications, Inc.
160 E. Virginia Street #290
San Jose, CA 95112-5876
1-408-286-8505 (voice)
1-408-287-8748 (fax)

Originated, designed, and printed in the United States of
America.

ISBN 1 85607 179 0

To all my loved ones,
family and friends,
especially my husband, Bob,
who incarnates Christ to me

Contents

Acknowledgments ix

Introduction xi

Season of Advent

First Sunday of Advent (A) 2

First Sunday of Advent (B). 4

First Sunday of Advent (C) 6

   Monday of First Week of Advent   8

   Tuesday of First Week of Advent   10

   Wednesday of First Week of Advent   12

   Thursday of First Week of Advent   14

   Friday of First Week of Advent   16

   Saturday of First Week of Advent   18

Second Sunday of Advent (A) 20

Second Sunday of Advent (B). 22

Second Sunday of Advent (C) 24

   Monday of Second Week of Advent   26

   Tuesday of Second Week of Advent   28

   Wednesday of Second Week of Advent   30

   Thursday of Second Week of Advent   32

   Friday of Second Week of Advent   34

   Saturday of Second Week of Advent   36

Third Sunday of Advent (A). 38

Third Sunday of Advent (B) 40

Third Sunday of Advent (C). 42

   Monday of Third Week of Advent   44

   Tuesday of Third Week of Advent   46

   Wednesday of Third Week of Advent   48

   Thursday of Third Week of Advent   50

   Friday of Third Week of Advent   52

Fourth Sunday of Advent (A) **54**

Fourth Sunday of Advent (B). **56**

Fourth Sunday of Advent (C). **58**

Weekday of Advent (December 17)   60

Weekday of Advent (December 18)   62

Weekday of Advent (December 19)   64

Weekday of Advent (December 20)   66

Weekday of Advent (December 21)   68

Weekday of Advent (December 22)   70

Weekday of Advent (December 23)   72

Weekday of Advent (December 24)

  — Morning Mass   74

Immaculate Conception (December 8) **76**

Season of Christmas

Christmas — Mass of the Vigil (ABC). **80**

Christmas — Mass at Midnight (ABC) **82**

Christmas — Mass at Dawn (ABC) **84**

Christmas — Mass during the Day (ABC) **86**

Second Day in Octave of Christmas

  (December 26)   88

Third Day in Octave of Christmas

  (December 27)   90

Fourth Day in Octave of Christmas

  (December 28)   92

Fifth Day in Octave of Christmas

  (December 29)   94

Sixth Day in Octave of Christmas

  (December 30)   96

Seventh Day in Octave of Christmas

  (December 31)   98

Sunday in Octave of Christmas, Holy Family (A) 100
Sunday in Octave of Christmas, Holy Family (B) 102
Sunday in Octave of Christmas, Holy Family (C) 104
Octave of Christmas, Solemnity of Mary,
    Mother of God (ABC) 106

    Christmas Weekday before Epiphany
        (January 2)   108
    Christmas Weekday before Epiphany
        (January 3)   110
    Christmas Weekday before Epiphany
        (January 4)   112
    Christmas Weekday before Epiphany
        (January 5)   114
    Christmas Weekday before Epiphany
        (January 6)   116
    Christmas Weekday before Epiphany
        (January 7)   118
Epiphany (ABC) 120

Baptism of the Lord (A) 122
Baptism of the Lord (B) 124
Baptism of the Lord (C) 126

Index of Lectionary References 129

Acknowledgments

Introduction

The Advent-Christmas-Epiphany season that we celebrate as Christians is not just an observance of events that happened long ago. It is not a sentimental birthday of the "baby Jesus." Nor is the season exclusively future oriented, watching and waiting for the coming of the exalted Christ at the end of time. The season is a celebration of God's self-disclosure in Jesus Christ, the eternal *Emmanuel*—God who was with the people in the past and who is with us now and for all time to come. In Jesus, God's love is made visible. Everything Jesus said, did, and suffered reveals God's love to us. The season takes its meaning from Christ's passion, death, resurrection, ascension, and sending of the Spirit. For three hundred years the church celebrated no other aspect of Christ than this paschal mystery. Our Christmas celebration takes its meaning from this mystery. The crib, the cross, and the crown are closely connected.

Advent is a time of joyful anticipation of the realization of God's promise. It is a grace-filled season of new hope, new life, and new love. There is a sense of urgency in Advent that wakes us up from our complacency. Advent should challenge us to prepare ourselves and our world for the full coming of the kingdom of peace and justice.

Christmas is a time to celebrate the fulfillment of God's promise, the one who took flesh in the womb of the Virgin Mary. The child is given the name "Jesus," meaning "God is with us" to save us from our sins. Christ is born so that we might be reborn to a life of grace. Christmas is the affirmation of *Emmanuel*, who is always present to his people. Our celebration is about more than the birth of a child; it is about the salvation of the world. Christmas challenges us to live the kind of life that God's kingdom demands now, with hope and promise for tomorrow.

Christmas is not just a day but a season that lasts twelve days. It continues through Epiphany and ends with the Baptism of the Lord, a celebration of God's faithfulness manifested to the whole world in Jesus Christ. Epiphany means a "recognition" of or "insight" into a reality of something. Epiphany is about a journey and the one who guides our quest to uncover the full meaning of Christ in our lives: the gift of God's love revealed through the Word, prayer, worship, and sacrament. For those who have the eyes to see, it is a time to perceive the signs of Christ's presence here and now—the ordinary and extraordinary appearances of the Lord in a star in the night sky, in strangers and visitors from afar, in families and loved ones, in light and life, in bread, wine and water, in Spirit and grace.

As we exchange gifts with our loved ones, we must also prepare ourselves for the true gift of God's love. Do we accept God's gift with gratitude? Do we proclaim the good news to others? How can we become more joyful, hopeful, faithful lovers of ourselves, God, and others? Are we watching and preparing for Christ's coming now and at the end of time? The preface for Advent reminds us to "Watch for the day" so that our hearts may be "filled with wonder and praise" when the Lord comes. Christ's coming will only be recognized by those who are alert to his appearance every day. May this season of Emmanuel fill you with the Lord's abiding presence.

Season of Advent

First Sunday of Advent (A)

Mt 24:37-44
   Isa 2:1-5; Ps 122; Rom 13:11-14

Keep awake therefore, for you do not know on what day your Lord is coming. — *Mt 24:42*

To Note

Advent (Latin: *aventus*, "coming") marks the beginning of the church's liturgical year. The season, consisting of the four weeks preceding the celebration of Christmas, has origins that date back to the fourth century. Advent is marked by joyful expectation of the Lord's threefold coming: his first coming in the flesh at his birth, his "second" coming at the end of time, and his coming in the Word and Spirit into our hearts to guide our actions. The season urges us to have constant vigilance as we watch and wait to identify the presence of Christ in our lives. Violet vestments remind to make a new beginning as Christ is reborn in our lives through repentance and grace.

To Understand

"Wake up!" the voice is insistent. "Zzz"—we turn over and pull the covers over our heads to shut out the morning light. "Wake up!" the voice persists. It is hard to rouse ourselves from our lethargy. Even when we are physically awake, there are times when we exist in the twilight, somewhere between daylight and darkness. We are like sleepwalkers, numb and unaware of the signs around us. The "deeds of darkness" have become all too familiar— crime, violence, jealousy, quarreling between individuals and nations. We have learned the ways of the world and walk in the paths that lead to conflict and warfare. We are

2

anesthetized to the pain and too paralyzed to act. We need prophets like Isaiah to wake us up to the ways of God that lead to peace. "Come, let us climb the Lord's mountain!" he says. Let us raise our sights above the shadow lands so we can gain a clearer view to see beyond the horizon where the light of God is rising.

Paul says the "hour" to wake from our sleep has arrived. Every moment is God's "time," the *kairos* moment of salvation. It happens when we least expect it. It sneaks up on us like a thief in the night. Though we are preoccupied by our daily tasks, plying our trades in the home, field, or city, salvation is ready to break into our lives. Jesus warns us to heed the message of Noah's day and not be carried away by the flood of destruction. We must be awake and put on "the Lord Jesus Christ." Fully clothed in the garments of salvation, we watch for the day not in fear but in joyful anticipation of its arrival.

To Consider

- What are the weapons of hostility in my life that need to be transformed into instruments of peace?
- What are the concerns of my community that I have ignored or neglected?
- What is God asking me to do?

To Pray

Light one candle of the Advent wreath and pray Psalm 122: God of Peace, I pray for our troubled cities, homes, and communities. Wake us up so they will become havens of peace and unity for the sake of us all.

First Sunday of Advent (B)

Mk 13:33-37
   Isa 63:16-17,19, 64:2-7; Ps 80; 1 Cor 1:3-9

And what I say to you I say to all: Keep awake. — Mk 13:37

To Note

The custom of lighting the Advent wreath originated in pre-Christian Germany and Scandinavia, where people celebrated the return of the sun after the long, dark winter. The wreath is made of a circle of evergreens with four candles representing the four weeks of Advent. The evergreens stand for life that endures in the midst of winter. The candles are a symbol of Christ, who breaks through the darkness with the light of his love. As the light of the wreath grows brighter, so does our expectation of God's promise to send a savior. Our prayers rekindle in us the desire to prepare the way for our rebirth in Christ.

To Understand

When we look forward to something with joyful expectation, it's hard when our hopes are dashed to the ground. It's easy to blame God for our troubles. "Where are you, God?" we ask. "You are our Father. Why did you let us down?" It may take a long while to realize that God has not abandoned us; we are the ones who have wandered from God. It isn't God who got us into this mess but our faithlessness to God's ways. God is not hiding nor asleep. We are the ones who are dormant. We need to rouse ourselves to God's presence. We must own our sins and call upon God's name, asking for deliverance and mercy. This change of heart means conversion from doubt and self-pity. It means humble recognition that God formed us

4

from the dust of the earth as a potter fashions a vessel. We are human receptacles, created to contain the gifts of God.

Paul gives thanks for the divine favors God graciously bestows upon the church. We are summoned to use these gifts to bring peace to our communities. That's a monumental task, but we don't have to do it on our own. God calls us into partnership with Jesus Christ to use God's gifts to work for peace. As we wait in hope, Jesus commands us: "Be constantly on the watch! Stay awake!" That doesn't mean sitting around dreaming of a better world. Jesus commissions us to be his servants in charge of the household. That's not someone else's duty. Each of us must take responsibility lest the enemy destroy what Christ has built. We must be ever watchful and dare not fall asleep on the job. Whether it is dusk, the dark of night, or early dawn, we must be alert to Christ's coming as in the full light of day.

To Consider

- What causes me to be discouraged?
- Have I ever thought that God has let me down?
- How have I failed God?
- What am I doing to help others experience God's presence and mercy?

To Pray

Light one candle of the Advent wreath and pray Psalm 80: Lord, let us turn to you. Show us your face and rouse us from our apathy. Strengthen us to work diligently to bring your reign upon the earth.

First Sunday of Advent (C)

Lk 21:25-28,34-36
  Jer 33:14-16; Ps 25; 1 Thess 3:12-4:2

Now when these things begin to take place, stand up and raise your heads, because your redemption is drawing near.
— Lk 21:28

To Note

The Advent calendar, which originated in Germany, consists of biblical scenes hidden behind little doors and opened each day. The custom of trimming a pine tree at Christmas also had its roots in Germany. The tree symbolized the tree of Paradise and was decorated with apples as a reminder of the "old" Adam, who fell into sin, and the "new" Adam, Jesus, who saved us. The Jesse tree tells the story of the spiritual family tree of Jesus Christ. Some symbols are the "apple" which tempted Adam and Eve; Jacob's ladder; Joseph's many-colored coat; the tablets of Moses' law; the harp of David (son of Jesse); Solomon's crown; Elijah's raven; and water for John the Baptist. All of these customs are useful in keeping the memory of Jesus alive in each generation of believers.

To Understand

We are often tempted to lose patience when our hopes and dreams are thwarted. When the Hebrew people were in exile in Babylon, their patience wore thin. The holy city of Jerusalem, the temple, the land, and the kingship were no more. With their past identity obliterated, they felt like the living dead. They doubted that God would fulfill the promises that gave them hope: "Your house and your kingdom shall be made sure forever." The prophet Jere-

6

miah tells us not to give up. Though David's family tree has been cut down, a green shoot will emerge from the dead stump, and life will begin again. The fall of a city, a ruler, or a nation does not mean life is over. Such disasters occur in every generation. Yet in the midst of life's hardships, it is difficult for us to understand God's ways. "Guide me in your way and teach me," we pray, "for you are God my Savior, for you I wait all the day."

Paul encourages the church to walk in ways that are pleasing to God. Though we can take comfort in the progress we have made in our spiritual lives, we know there is more work to be done. When we are tempted to get discouraged, Jesus tells us, "Stand up straight and raise your heads." Our whole world may be shaken by wars and natural disasters outside ourselves and by self-indulgence and addictions within. Such things should not make us fearful and bowed down. By patient and prayerful watching for our coming salvation, we can lift up our eyes and stand secure before the Lord. Kings and kingdoms may pass away, but the Word of God stands firm forever.

To Consider

- Am I tempted to forget God's promises when things do not go well?
- Do I comfort others when they are discouraged?
- What am I doing to guide my family along God's paths?

To Pray

Light one candle of the Advent wreath and pray Psalm 25: Lord, help me raise my heart and voice to you. Guide me in the way of peace and justice. Show me the path to truth.

Monday of First Week of Advent

Mt 8:5-11
   Isa 2:1-5; Ps 122

Note: In Year A, Isa 4:2-6 is read when Isa 2:1-5 is used on First
Sunday of Advent.

*Lord, I am not worthy to have you come under my roof; but
only speak the word, and my servant will be healed.*
— Mt 8:8

To Note

The U.S. Catholic Bishops spoke on the issues of peace
and war in their 1983 pastoral letter, "The Challenge of
Peace: God's Promise and Our Response." They declared:
"As disciples and children of God it is our task to seek for
ways in which to make the forgiveness, justice and mercy,
and love of God visible in a world where violence and
enmity are too often the norm." Saying "no" to war is not
enough. All church, political, and military leaders and
ordinary citizens must say "yes" to peace and justice.

To Understand

The prophet Isaiah has a vision of the joyful, peaceable
kingdom of God. Military and political leaders won't dic-
tate terms for war and peace. The just God imposes demili-
tarization and disarmament. Universal peace is accepted
by all people as they exchange their weapons of war for
tools of peace. God washes away the blood and guilt from
the city and creates a sanctuary where all are secure. The
messianic "branch of the Lord" brings salvation to all the
faithful. The people rejoice as they process to the city of
God, *Shalom Jerushalaim*, "the city of peace."

The glorious vision of the future is interrupted by the day-to-day reality of suffering. A man in the military approaches Jesus with a compassionate request, "My servant is paralyzed and is suffering greatly." Jesus' answer is immediate, "I will come." Jesus is eager to respond to our needs whether or not we deserve his favor. Yet the soldier demurs. He knows what authority means. His word of command is sufficient to control his legion and his servants. But the centurion knows that Jesus has greater authority. "Speak but the word and my servant will be healed," this stalwart soldier implores.

In the midst of heartache and distress, we recognize our own powerlessness. We can only appeal to a greater power. Humbly we approach the altar of the Lord, the place of refuge and healing. Many others come from the east and the west to stand beside us at the table. For a moment, we are gathered at the eternal banquet in the kingdom of God. We pray for ourselves, "Lord, I am not worthy to receive you, but only say the word and I shall be healed." We pray for the healing of our relatives and friends, "Peace be within you," we whisper. "I will come," Jesus replies.

To Consider

- Do I pray for peace and healing in my home and community?
- Do I believe that I have to earn God's favors?
- Can I accept God's mercy regardless of my feelings of unworthiness?

To Pray

Pray Psalm 122: Lord, give me joy as I go to your house of prayer. Help me to be confident that I will find peace and healing at your table.

Tuesday of First Week of Advent

Lk 10:21-24
   Isa 11:1-10; Ps 72

For I tell you that many prophets and kings desired to see what you see, but did not see it, and to hear what you hear, but did not hear it. — Lk 10:24

To Note

The traditional seven spiritual gifts of the Holy Spirit are wisdom, understanding, counsel, fortitude, knowledge, piety, and fear of the Lord. Saints Justin Martyr, Augustine, and Thomas Aquinas developed a theology as to how these gifts complete and perfect the virtues of those who receive them. The gifts of the Spirit can never be catalogued as there is no end to God's gifts. Other lists of the gifts of the Spirit are Romans 12:6-8; 1 Corinthians 12:4-11; Ephesians 4:11.

To Understand

Beneath the cold, crusty ground, life is stirring, though soundless and invisible to the human eye. In the dead of winter, when everything seems barren and lifeless, a green shoot breaks forth from the womb of the earth. It is a metaphor for all of life, at once delicate and vigorous. So too is the paradox of God's kingdom: the child can put a hand in the cobra's den fearing no harm. The predator and prey—wolf and lamb, lion and calf—all dwell together in harmony. Such is the rule of the Messiah of God, who governs with power and might yet with tender mercy. Instead of royal garments, God's agent is girt with justice and fidelity. He does not judge by outward appearance but with God's gifts of wisdom and holiness. When the poor and lowly cry out and no one hears or helps them, the Messiah is there to save. With him, all peoples of the earth live securely in justice and peace.

At times, this seems like an impossible dream. We have trouble believing the promises. Where is the one who will lead us to salvation? In the wintry seasons of our lives, we fail to notice that the root of Jesse buds and blossoms. The pledge to David is fulfilled in Jesus. This mystery has been revealed not to the wise and powerful but to the little ones, men and women of faith. Jesus blesses our eyes so we can see the signs of God's reign, which those who are wise in the ways of the world cannot perceive. He blesses our ears so we can hear the good news of the Gospel and recognize the cries of the poor. Because we are blessed, it is our responsibility to use the gifts God gives us to build a better world. When we live in awesome fear of God's ways, justice will flourish in our time. There will be fullness of peace forever. We rejoice at the coming of God's reign.

To Consider

- Have I used God's gifts God to build a peaceable world?
- In my experience, how does knowledge lead to understanding?
- How does wisdom offer counsel?
- In what ways does a Christian use strength?
- What do holiness and fear of God mean in the world today?

To Pray

Pray Psalm 72: O God, help us to govern your people with justice. Give us the wisdom to help the poor and afflicted who have no one to help them. Bless all the nations of the earth with peace and happiness.

Wednesday of First Week of Advent

Mt 15:29-37
   Isa 25:6-10; Ps 23

Where are we to get enough bread in the desert to feed so great a crowd? — Mt 15:33

To Note

It is estimated that between five hundred million and one billion people in the world suffer from hunger. Each year twenty million people, the majority of them children, die of hunger or related diseases. In 1946 UNICEF, United Nations Children's Fund, was established to carry out war relief in Europe. Today it is concerned with the welfare of children living in developing nations. (Source: Church World Service, P.O. Box 968, Elkhart, IN 46515). The Campaign for Human Development is the Catholic church's effort to end poverty and injustice in America (United States Catholic Conference, 3211 Fourth St. NE, Washington, DC 20017).

To Understand

When God's people gather in true worship, the veil that obscures our vision of God's kingdom is lifted. Together we sit at a messianic feast of rich food and choice wine. Sadness and mourning are no more; all tears are wiped away. Together we cross the borders of doubt and despair and climb to the mountain top where the air is pure. There we can walk, talk, and dance for joy. "This is the Lord for whom we have waited; let us be glad and rejoice in his salvation!"

Yet we know that in this world there are plenty of tears to wipe. The sick, wounded, powerless, and voiceless cry out for mercy. Their desperation moves Jesus to the depths of his being. Then he turns to us. We cannot stand by as idle observers. "The people are hungry," he tells us. "What can we do about it?" we look for a way out. Where can we find enough food to satisfy all *those* people? He doesn't expect us to pay for it, does he? How can we make a difference? We're so few and they're so many. We shrug our shoulders and scratch our heads. We look helplessly around, hoping someone will get us off the hook. Jesus still looks at us. "What is in your hands?" he asks. "Nothing. A little. Just a *few* loaves of bread, some *small* fish. It's not enough." Jesus ignores our weak excuses. He asks everyone to sit down as at a banquet table. He gives thanks for what he has received. Then he breaks the bread that has been offered and hands it to us. "You give it to them," he says. Full of skepticism we share the gift we have received. "Take and eat." Wonder of wonders! Not only is there enough, there is an abundance. We fall on our knees in gratitude. "You spread a table before me. Only goodness and kindness follow me all the days of my life."

To Consider

- Am I aware of the suffering of those around me, or am I deaf and blind to their plight?
- Do I share what I have with others?
- Do I trust God to supply whatever I lack?

To Pray

Pray Psalm 23: Lord, be our guide in this valley of tears. Help everyone to find a place at your table of plenty so that we can live in your goodness and kindness forever.

Thursday of First Week of Advent

Mt 7:21,24-27
   Isa 26:1-6; Ps 118

Everyone then who hears these words of mine and acts on them will be like a wise man who built his house on rock. —
Mt 7:24

To Note

Relief agencies and the government supply aid to victims of natural catastrophes such as tornados, hurricanes, earthquakes, fires, or floods. Homelessness is equally catastrophic to society. Short-term measures do not address the larger problems such as lack of jobs and affordable housing. Some agencies that provide creative efforts in the area of homelessness and related problems are: Habitat for Humanity, 121 Habitat St., Americus, GA 31709; National Low Income Housing Coalition, 1-12 14th St. NE, Suite 1500, Washington, DC 20005; Network, 806 Rhode Island Ave. NE, Washington, DC 20018.

To Understand

When the world has been shaken by war and destruction, the prophet urges: "Trust in the Lord forever! For the Lord is an eternal rock." It's hard to trust in anything when in exile, far from our homeland. Though we weep for what has been lost, we cling to the hope that one day we will sing a song in the land of promise. But now is not a time for songs. Now we need to act. The nation is devastated; the great city brought low. Foolishly, we have put our trust in rulers and have been disappointed. It is time to learn our lessons. We must be firm in our determination to live in peace, justice, and fidelity. We must get to work.

Jesus breaks into our daydreaming. He tells us that it is not enough to call out, "Lord, Lord." The ones who will enter the kingdom of God are those who do the will of God. If we hear Jesus' words, we must put them into practice. Then when the storms of life threaten us, we will not be moved. If we hear Jesus' words and refuse to put them into action, we are foolish. Our foundation is only sand. Our world will be turned upside down; it will collapse and end in utter ruin. We must be wise and build our homes, our cities, our nations, our churches on the "eternal rock" who is the Lord. Walls and ramparts must be constructed to protect the weak who have been trampled upon by the powerful. The gates of the city and the temple must be opened wide so that the poor and needy can find refuge. There must be a place for everyone who is homeless and table-less. Then all who enter our gates will give thanks-giving and praise, "I will give thanks to you, for you have answered me and have been my savior. Blessed is he who comes in the name of the Lord."

To Consider

- Have I built my spiritual house on rock or on sand?
- Has this made a difference during the storms of life?
- How can I help others rebuild their lives in times of crises?

To Pray

Pray Psalm 118: Lord, I give you thanks for being a refuge in time of need. Help me to open the gates of justice to those in need.

Friday of First Week of Advent

Mt 9:27-31
  Isa 29:17-24; Ps 27

When he entered the house, the blind men came to him; and Jesus said to them, "Do you believe that I am able to do this?" They said to him, "Yes, Lord." — Mt 9:28

To Note

Faith can include times of hope and trust and also times of questions and doubt. Speaking on the subject of faith, the *Catechism of the Catholic Church* declares that "even though enlightened by him in whom it believes, faith is often lived in darkness and can be put to the test. The world we live in often seems very far from the one promised us by faith. Our experiences of evil and suffering, injustice, and death, seem to contradict the Good News; they can shake our faith and become a temptation against it" (#164).

To Understand

So many things can cause times of darkness in our lives. Darkness comes unannounced in the death of a loved one, a serious illness, the loss of a job, the end of a marriage or relationship, or when our children break our hearts. It leaps out of the shadows when crime, alcohol, and other drugs invade our lives. It descends as a black cloud when we are innocent and accused of wrongdoing. It blocks out the sun when we are abused, betrayed, cheated, or violated. At such times we grope our way in what seems a perpetual night of confusion and gloom. We feel like the walking dead. We feel anger, shame, or guilt. We cannot see, hear, or speak. We have no joy. We wonder if the sun will ever shine again. Will faith and hope return? Deep within we utter a soundless plea, "Have pity on us."

Somehow, somewhere in the murky shadows a ray of hope begins to shine. Though we still cannot see the Lord, we know that he is there. Jesus speaks, "Are you confident I can do this?" he asks. A tiny spark of faith flickers, and we have the courage to say, "Yes, Lord." We feel a gentle touch. "Because of your faith it shall be done to you, " he says. Finally the dawn comes, perhaps slowly, sometimes swiftly. The cloud lifts and we see the light of day. "The Lord is my light and salvation," we rejoice as we contemplate the mystery, in awe of God's infinite power and limitless love. We feel safe and have new courage. The tyrant of despair is gone and we are no longer afraid. New life returns and we can look forward to the future with faith and confidence. We cannot keep the good news to ourselves. Many others still dwell in darkness, waiting for someone to wake them from their nightmares. We must tell them: "Be brave! We have seen the work of the Lord in our midst. Wait for the Lord with courage."

To Consider

- When have I been blind and deaf to the Lord's presence?
- What helped me to see and hear?
- Whom might I help by sharing my story with them?

To Pray

Pray Psalm 27: Lord, when I am afraid, you are my light and refuge. Help me to wait for your coming in times of darkness.

Saturday of First Week of Advent

Mt 9:35-10:1,6-8
   Isa 30:19-21,23-26; Ps 147

The harvest is plentiful, but the laborers are few; therefore ask the Lord of the harvest to send out laborers into his harvest. — Mt 9:37-38

To Note

The majority of people in countries where hunger exists want to support themselves with farming and other productive work, but they are often deprived of the basic necessities: land, water, tools, draft animals, credit, and markets for their crops. All over the world, people are working to end hunger and eliminate its causes. For information, publications, videos, films, and speakers contact: Catholic Relief Services 209 West Fayette Street, Baltimore, MD 21201; Oxfam America, 115 Broadway, Boston, MA 02116; or Bread for the World, 802 Rhode Island Avenue, NE Washington, DC 20018.

To Understand

God hears and answers us when we cry out for mercy. When we are hurt and broken-hearted, God binds up our wounds. When we are hungry, God gives us bread to eat and satisfies our thirst. When there is drought, God sends the rain. Streams of water pour forth from the lofty mountains to nourish the seed that has been sown in the ground. The animals graze in spacious meadows. There is no famine because the crops are rich and abundant. Sound like a dream? A fairy-tale? Utopia? The reality of our world doesn't match the lovely picture drawn by the prophet. People suffer injustice and wrongdoing. They die from wars, sickness and disease, malnourishment, and drought. Soil is depleted, crops fail, livestock perish. At such times, it seems that God doesn't hear our cries or care.

Jesus walks into our lives, our towns and villages, and our churches. He sees the people worn out with exhaustion, struggling to survive in a harsh world. They are like sheep without a shepherd, with no teacher to lead or guide them. At the sight of suffering, his heart is moved with pity. "The harvest is plentiful, but there are not enough harvesters," Jesus tells us. "Does he mean us?" we wonder. We have no experience, no skills, no power to change things. We can't bear to look. We hide our eyes and walk away. Then we hear his voice, "This is the way to my kingdom," he says. "Walk in it. Follow the straight path. Don't turn right or left." Jesus summons and challenges us. He gives us authority over evil, empowers us to mend and heal. "Go!" he commands. "Go to the lost sheep and announce the good news to them. Cure them, heal them. Expel the demons of sickness, dispair and death." Jesus gives us a gift that we must give to others.

To Consider

- What are the needs of my community?
- What resources are available to accomplish these goals?
- What gifts do I have that I can share with others?

To Pray

Pray Psalm 147: Gracious God, help us to show compassion to the wounded and brokenhearted. Give us the wisdom to heal them.

Second Sunday of Advent (A)

Mt 3:1-12
   Isa 11:1-10; Ps 72; Rom 15:4-9

Prepare the way of the Lord,
  make his paths straight. — Mt 3:3

To Note

Advent is not a penitential season like Lent; it is a time to prepare our hearts to receive the Lord with joy. The sacrament of reconciliation expresses our gratitude to God for sending Jesus to save us from our sins. Advent is a time to examine our relationship with God and others. Am I grateful for God's love, especially for forgiveness of my sins? Am I bitter toward anyone: family, friends, neighbors, or co-workers? Have I forgiven those who have injured me? Am I willing to smooth the rough way even when it is not easy? Advent is a time to make a new beginning. Am I willing to say yes to God's invitation of grace?

To Understand

The land lay in such ruin that it appeared to be a stump of a decayed tree. Like the dying tree, the nation's ruler was weak and corrupt, only too willing to take the easy way out. He would even compromise with the enemy if it meant saving his own neck. No matter how bleak the situation, the prophet Isaiah does not give up hope. The prophet is confident that new growth is possible even from apparently lifeless roots. A powerful Messiah will reign in place of the impotent ruler, and paradise is restored. In God's reign, the weak and powerless are not harmed by the strong and mighty. As incredible as it might seem, all live as one in God's glorious dwelling place.

Paul encourages us to learn a lesson from the past. If we want to live in perfect harmony with one another, we must act in accord with the spirit of Christ. Like Christ, we must be a servant to all. We need to have hope and patience and do much hard work if we want to see the goal fulfilled. But we are not so sure the dream is possible. The only time we've seen the wolf laying down with the lamb is when the lamb is between its teeth.

John the Baptist wakes us up. Now is no time for daydreams. John doesn't ask us politely to reform our lives. He demands it. His images are less utopian than Isaiah's. There's no time to nurse a fruitless tree. The ax is already laid to the root. The ones that have not born good fruit will be cut down and burned in unquenchable fire. There's no use hiding or running away. It is time to make a decision. We can't tell lies or give lip-service saying we have changed our lives when we have not. There must be some evidence of our conversion. We can't pride ourselves on being Catholic, Baptist, or Presbyterian. Nor can we depend on the faith of our grandmothers or grandfathers to save us. God has no grandchildren, only sons and daughters who are faithful to the Gospel of Christ.

To Consider

- How am I preparing my heart for the Lord's coming?
- Is my life different today than it was yesterday? Will it be different tomorrow?

To Pray

Light two candles of the Advent wreath and pray Psalm 72: O God, may you rule from sea to sea with justice and peace. Rescue the poor and afflicted so all peoples of the earth may find blessing in you.

Second Sunday of Advent (B)

Mk 1:1-8
  Isa 40:1-5,9-11; Ps 85; 2 Pet 3:8-14

*The one who is more powerful than I is coming after me; I
am not worthy to stoop down and untie the thong of his
sandals. — Mk 1:7*

To Note

The *Catechism of the Catholic Church* declares that "*everyone
is called to enter the kingdom*" (543). God's reign, first
announced to the children of Israel, is intended to accept
people of all nations. Jesus is sent by God to preach the
good news to the "*poor and lowly*," those who accept it with
humble hearts (544). Jesus invites "*sinners* to the table of
the kingdom." He calls everyone to "that conversion without which one cannot enter the kingdom, but shows them
in word and deed his Father's boundless mercy for
them..." (545).

To Understand

Waiting for either good or bad news can be equally stress-
ful. Anticipating the mail, a report card, a doctor's report,
a birth or a death fills us with anxiety. God's people were
in exile, and they anxiously awaited freedom. It was get-
ting harder to maintain hope. Some had given up and had
settled down to making a life for themselves in a foreign
land. Others compromised, buying into all the trappings of
the "good life." Isaiah urges them to remember God's
faithfulness. If God led a band of slaves out of Egypt,
couldn't God do the same for them? Like a shepherd
guiding his flock, God will lead them home again.

For us, with our human limitations, one day of waiting can seem like a thousand years. Peter says that time is different for God. God's promises will be fulfilled, perhaps not by our calendars and watches but with guaranteed fidelity. God has plenty of time to wait for each one of us to repent and come home. As when welcoming a loved one home, kindness and truth shall meet; justice and peace shall kiss.

John the Baptizer knows that he is the messenger of good news, but he is not the message. He has led the people as far as he can take them. He can go no further. With great humility, John accepts his role as servant and not master. John is happy just to play a part. Like a supporting actor, he knows when it is time to step back and allow the leading man to take center stage. He has waited a long time for this event. With joy he announces, "Clear a pathway! Make straight the way of the Lord." John is God's mighty voice, yet Jesus' words and deeds are more powerful than John's. Where John stresses judgment, Jesus speaks of salvation. John preaches a baptism of repentance, but at Jesus' coming, we are immersed in the refining fire of the Holy Spirit. The world waited a long time to hear this good news. It is well worth the wait!

To Consider

- How do I use my time as I await the Lord's coming?
- Am I willing to be a servant to God's people, or do I want to be their master?
- In what ways can I serve with humility and love?

To Pray

Light two candles of the Advent wreath and pray Psalm 85: Lord, help me to hear what you proclaim. Let me see your kindness and salvation as I wait in hope for you.

Second Sunday of Advent (C)

Lk 3:1-6
  Bar 5:1-9; Ps 126; Phil 1:4-6,8-11

Every valley shall be filled,
  and every mountain and hill shall be made low,
and the crooked shall be made straight,
  and the rough ways made smooth. — Lk 3:5

To Note

The four *cardinal* (of main importance) virtues are prudence, justice, fortitude, and temperance. Prudence is
related to prayerful discernment of the true good in every
circumstance and of the right means to accomplish it.
Justice is the determination to give to God and to others
what is their due. Fortitude strengthens our ability to
overcome obstacles and resist temptation. Temperance, or
moderation, is self-control over one's appetites. These
virtues help us to lead a whole and moral life (*Catechism of
the Catholic Church* 1806-9).

To Understand

In times of suffering we wait in darkness, patiently watching for the rising of the sun. In the new light of day, we can
see things more clearly. Then we can take off our mourning clothes, and wrap ourselves in a cloak of God's glory.
Though the enemy has left us weak and shattered, we
have confidence that God will bring us to the place where
we can be safe and secure. Sometimes it seems like a
dream. Other times it is a nightmare. We have looked too
long into the depths and gorges of despair. We are tempted
to doubt God's promises. We need a reminder of the great
things that God has done for us.

24

Paul knows what it is like to suffer the loss of everything that he holds dear. Yet behind the dark prison walls he can still say, "Rejoice!" Paul prays for courage not only for himself but for all of us. Because he has learned to value the things that really matter, he is certain that we will too. God is faithful. Even though we lose sight of God's action in our lives, God remembers us. God knows how hard we have labored on behalf of the Gospel. The good work begun in us will be brought to completion.

John the Baptist knows suffering and failure too, yet he never loses courage as he delivers God's message, "Make ready the way of the Lord!" Some don't want to hear that kind of news. They are comfortable with the way things are. Though forces threaten to destroy him, John continues to proclaim a "baptism of repentance." Like Paul and John, we need the courage to make the right choices. We need faith that Christ will fill all the empty places in our lives, that we can overcome any obstacle, and that we can find our way through the twists and turns of life. Then we will see the salvation of God and rejoice at Christ's coming. Though we went forth weeping, we will return rejoicing!

To Consider

- How can I exercise the virtue of prudence this Advent?
- Where do I need courage and self-control?
- How am I practicing justice?

To Pray

Light two candles of the Advent wreath and pray Psalm 126: Lord, in times of struggle, help me to remember your love and fidelity. Fill me with joy so that I can tell everyone of the good things you have done for me.

Monday of Second Week of Advent

Lk 5:17-26
  Isa 35:1-10; Ps 85

Which is easier, to say, "Your sins are forgiven you," or to say, "Stand up and walk"? — Lk 5:23

To Note

In 1950, the General Assembly of the United Nations proclaimed December 10 as Human Rights Day to promote and encourage respect for "human rights and fundamental freedom." The church is also concerned for the physical, as well as the spiritual, well-being of all people. The *Catechism of the Catholic Church* asserts that society must help in the attainment of those "living-conditions" that allow its citizens "to grow and reach maturity: food and clothing, housing, health care, basic education, employment, and social assistance" (2288).

To Understand

Isaiah fills the exiled people with hope of returning to their homeland. But is it a realistic hope? Most of them have grown old in exile. Some are sick and weak. Can they survive the long trek home? Will they find an oasis in the burning desert? Hands tremble and knees go weak at the incredible prospect. The prophet tells them, "Be strong, fear not!" God will provide a straight highway through the wilderness. Streams of water will burst forth in the wasteland. Flowers will bloom in abundance. No beast will prey on the helpless ones. Eyes blind to God's salvation and ears deaf to God's mercy will be opened. Though paralyzed by fear, we can stand up and walk to freedom, filled with joy once again. Together we enter Zion singing.

Through his word and works, Jesus fills people with new life. The sick recover in mind, body, and spirit. People go to great lengths to bring their loved ones to Jesus for healing. When there are obstacles in their paths, they even climb to the roof tops. Everyone is surprised to see a paralyzed man being lowered through the ceiling. Jesus is more amazed at the people's faith. He understands how unforgiveness, bitterness, and anger have kept them in bondage, and he forgives any wrongdoing they have done. The "holy" people see this as an affront to God. How can anyone but God forgive sins? "Which is easier," Jesus asks, "to forgive or to heal someone?" "Oh, healing is much easier than forgiving," we say to ourselves. Jesus knows how blind and deaf we can be to God's kindness. "Get up and walk!" he tells the wounded. We are full of awe and give praise to God for the incredible things we have seen. But we cannot stop there. Jesus invites us to be instruments of reconciliation, to say those three little words, "I forgive you," to those who hurt us. When we set one another free, we can both walk and leap with joy.

To Consider

- Whom do I need to forgive today? Can I offer forgiveness freely?
- How has society crippled people by not providing the basic necessities which give human dignity?
- What is my parish doing to bring healing?

To Pray

Pray Psalm 85: O God, come and save all who have lost hope. Help our land to yield a harvest of justice so that all may walk in peace and truth.

Tuesday of Second Week of Advent

Mt 18:12-14
   Isa 40:1-11; Ps 96

*It is not the will of your Father in heaven that one of these
little ones should be lost. — Mt 18:14*

To Note

The feast of Our Lady of Guadalupe commemorates four
appearances of the Blessed Virgin (December 9-12, 1531)
on a hill of Tepayac near Mexico City to a poor man named
Juan Diego. The Virgin told him to bear a message to the
bishop requesting a church be built there in her honor. As
proof that the message was authentic, roses bloomed in
mid-winter. Juan Diego wrapped the flowers in his cloak
(*tilma*) and took them to the bishop. When the cloak was
opened, there appeared the image of a young woman
dressed as an Aztec princess surrounded by rays of light.
Within two generations, eight million Aztecs converted to
Christianity. Known to the Aztecs as "Tecoatlaxope,"
meaning "she will crush the serpent of stone," she was
given the name "de Guadalupe" by the Spaniards. The
feast of Our Lady of Guadalupe, patroness and "Empress
of the Americas," is celebrated on December 12.

To Understand

When all seems lost, the prophet speaks a word of comfort.
Isaiah doesn't point out our sins. He knows that we have
paid the price for them several times over. Guilt, shame,
and alienation have exacted a heavy toll. Isaiah says to
open our eyes and we will see the God who comes to save
us, not as judge and ruler but as gentle shepherd who leads
the flock to safe pasture.

"What do you think about this?" Jesus asks. "Which of you, if you had one hundred sheep and one of them wanders away, would leave the others and go in search of the stray?" This must be a trick question. If a sheep is crazy enough to leave the flock where it's safe and secure, it is its own fault if it gets in trouble. Why risk ninety-nine cautious and intelligent sheep to go after one that is foolhardy? It isn't practical or economical. Who would do a thing like that? Jesus says, "God would." God is a shepherd who cares for the whole flock, even the one who goes astray.

"Not fair!" we pout. We have always been faithful. We're smart enough to know where we belong. We're not responsible for the wrong choices someone else makes. Then we remember our children, brothers, sisters, and friends who have wandered away from God. We recall all the times we strayed and God welcomed us home. Maybe there is cause for rejoicing. If it is God's plan that no one comes to grief, shouldn't it be our goal too? Perhaps it is time to take some risks and go search for the lost. We hope, too, that the rest of the faithful flock will join us.

To Consider

- Have I reached out with compassion to the alienated members of my church?
- Have I taken time to listen to their story?
- Do I welcome them with open arms when they return?

To Pray

Pray or *sing* Psalm 96: Lord, I want to sing a new song to you, a song filled with rejoicing. I want to bless your name day after day, announcing your salvation to all people.

Wednesday of Second Week of Advent

Mt 11:28-30
  Isa 40:25-31; Ps 103

Come to me, all you that are weary and are carrying heavy burdens, and I will give you rest. — Mt 11:28

To Note

The *Catechism of the Catholic Church* states that justice is a "moral virtue," often represented in the sacred Scriptures as impartial and unbiased conduct toward others. Biblical justice consists of "the constant and firm will to give their due to God and neighbor." Justice disposes people to "respect the rights of each and to establish in human relationships the harmony that promotes equity with regard to persons and to the common good" (1807).

To Understand

When we are weary of life's burdens, we stagger under a load too heavy to carry alone. When we sin, we are weighed down by shame and guilt. We don't know where to turn for relief. We have so many problems in marriage, with children, on the job, or with finances. They seem like a heavy yoke that will crush us. We can barely lift our heads. We feel like oppressed slaves with our necks in the harness. Our rights are disregarded, and no one seems to hear our pleas. We look for justice to redress the wrongs done to us, but the law seems to work against the innocent instead of for them. We look to the "wise and learned" of the world—lawyers, doctors, psychologists and other professionals—but feel ignorant when we cannot understand their clever arguments and complicated "legalese." We look to the church for help, but sometimes the "holy ones" make us feel like outsiders. At such times, the pathway to God seems inaccessible. God seems far away or absent. We may think that God doesn't care. Who will help us carry the load or make our pain less severe, our burden less troublesome? Where can we turn for help?

Isaiah tells us to lift our eyes to the Holy One who has created all things. God's wisdom and justice are beyond human scrutiny. God does not grow weary of doing good for the weak and faint-hearted. Neither does God judge us according to our sins. When we put our hope in God, our strength is renewed. We can walk and not grow tired. We can run and not collapse. Like an eagle, we soar high above our troubles.

Jesus understands how wearisome life can be. He knows what it is like to feel pain and rejection. Jesus will not spurn our cries for help. He invites all who are shackled and oppressed to come to him to find rest. Jesus is a humble teacher who guides us gently on the pathway to God. Obedience to his word is not a crushing obligation but the life-giving good news of salvation. Jesus is a servant of love who lifts the weight from our shoulders. Supported by Jesus, our burdens are easier to carry because he shares the load.

To Consider

- Who has helped me carry my burdens in time of need?
- Have I helped someone carry his/hers?
- How can I help those who are worn out by life's trials?

To Pray

Pray Psalm 103: Holy One, help me to remember your kindness and compassion. Thank you for forgiving, healing, and blessing me when I have been brought low.

Thursday of Second Week of Advent

Mt 11:11-15
 Isa 41:13-20; Ps 145

Truly I tell you, among those born of women no one has arisen greater than John the Baptist; yet the least in the kingdom of heaven is greater than he" — Mt 11:11

To Note

In the Bible, a prophet (Hebrew: *nabi*) is one who speaks on behalf of God. Prophets addressed social evil and religious corruption and offered hope to despairing people. Prophets are persecuted by those who refuse to hear God's message. Classic prophecy is associated with the "literary prophets" who emerged in the eighth century before Christ (Isaiah, Jeremiah, Ezekiel, Amos, Hosea, etc.). John the Baptist is the last and greatest of Israel's prophets. Paul says the gift of prophecy is given to the whole church for the "common good" for their "upbuilding and encouragement and consolation" (1 Cor 12:7; 14:3).

To Understand

When we feel alienated from God and society, it seems as though we are in exile. Having lost our identity, we feel as low as "maggots" and "worms." We need someone to give us hope. The prophet Isaiah speaks a word of consolation from the Lord, "Fear not, I will help you." God grasps us by the hand and pulls us out of our despair. Though we feel weak and ineffective, God makes us as powerful as a double-edged sickle. The obstacles that loomed like mountains before us are all brought low. Our troubles are blown away like chaff in the wind. Rivers of mercy flood the wasteland of our lives. We are awestruck and filled with wonder, "Who could do this incredible thing?" When we see it with our own eyes, we understand that it is God, the Holy One, who has done this.

John the Baptist appears in our wilderness with a fiery message: "Repent! God's kingdom is at hand!" God sends John as a messenger to prepare the way for the coming of Christ. John is the new Elijah, who has the courage to call people to fidelity to God's Word. But when John is locked in prison for speaking the truth, he doubts his own warning of the coming of God's refining fire. John wonders about Jesus, "Could this be the Messiah who comes with mercy rather than judgment?" Jesus knows that John is a powerful witness. The prophet is not a reed blowing this way and that before every changing wind. Jesus says, "History has not seen a greater man than John the Baptist." We wonder how anyone can live up to a reputation like that. Then Jesus looks at us, nobodies from nowhere. He says, "The least one of you born into God's reign through baptism is greater than John." Amazing as it seems, it is up to us to speak God's Word to those who feel weak and powerless. Like Isaiah, John, and Jesus, we can turn the deserts of life into springs of living water.

To Consider

- In what ways am I called to be a prophet?
- Have I had the courage to speak in spite of opposition?
- Who most needs to hear the good news today?

To Pray

Pray Psalm 145: O my God and King, help me to proclaim your mercy and compassion and bless you for all your good works. Your reign will endure for all ages.

Friday of Second Week of Advent

Mt 11:16-19
  Isa 48:17-19; Ps 1

But to what will I compare this generation? — Mt 11:16

To Note:

The Ten Commandments (Hebrew: *Dabar*, "words"), known also as the "Decalogue," were given to Moses by God on Mt. Sinai. Roman Catholics and Lutherans follow the arrangement of the commandments found in Deuteronomy 5:6-15. Jews, Eastern Orthodox, and other Protestants follow the list in Exodus 20:2-11. The first three laws have to do with the love and worship of Yahweh, who liberated Israel from slavery. As God's covenant people, we remain free by acting with justice toward others as expressed in the last seven commands. Jesus sums up the whole law as love of God and neighbor (Mt 22:37-40).

To Understand

God is a merciful liberator who acts to save us from bondage. God is our teacher who shows us how to live in freedom. Because we close our ears and refuse to obey God's words, we pay the price. We are like exiles, cut off from our ancestral roots. We feel blotted out from the Lord's presence. Isaiah speaks on God's behalf. Though far from the promised land, God has not forgotten us. If we listen to God once more, we will recover all we have lost. The ancient promises made to Abraham of a land, descendants, and blessings will be ours. The only requirement is to unite our will to God's.

Jesus knows how fickle we are. One moment we're eager to do God's will. The next, we close our ears and hearts and follow our own ways. Jesus recites a little verse from Aesop's fables to describe our behavior. We are like spoiled children whom no one can satisfy. In good times, when the music bids us to join in the dance of life, we stubbornly refuse. When we suffer the consequence of our misdeeds, we refuse to acknowledge our responsibility or lament our sins. Jesus and John are sent by God, but we refuse to listen to their message. John calls the people to repentance, but because he lives such an ascetic lifestyle, everyone says he is crazy. Jesus welcomes sinners to the table, and people say he is a glutton and a drunkard.

We are no different than the people of John's and Jesus' day. We ask, why give the best years of your life and shut yourself up in a convent or monastery? Why become a lay missionary? Why not stay here and work with your own? At other times we ask, who are all "those" people coming to "our" church? They don't belong at the table with the rest of us "good" people. Jesus knows how hypocritical we can be. He and John are children of divine wisdom who will justify their actions through their words and works.

To Consider

- Am I judgmental of other people's conduct?
- Am I able to work alongside those who are different than myself?
- What are John and Jesus telling me? Am I listening?

To Pray

Pray Psalm 1: Lord, if I follow your ways I will walk by your light. Help me to meditate on your law so that I will yield good fruit in all the seasons of my life.

Saturday of Second Week of Advent

Mt 17:10-13
   Sir 48:1-4,9-11; Ps 80

I tell you that Elijah has already come, and they did not recognize him, but they did to him whatever they pleased. So also the Son of Man is about to suffer at their hands.
— *Mt 17:12*

To Note

There are some special heroes whom we can use as models of faith during Advent. Francis Xavier, Jesuit missionary, traveled thousands of miles in harrowing conditions to preach the Gospel to the East Indies and India. He died before reaching his goal to evangelize China. Ambrose, Doctor of the Church, was a fierce defender of the faith. He is considered an exemplar for bishops: holy, learned and courageous. Lucy, whose name means "light," was a martyr of the fourth century, burned and stabbed to death for wanting to remain chaste. John of the Cross, Doctor of the Church, suffered in his attempts to reform the Carmelite Order. Like Teresa of Avila, John became a great mystic and spiritual writer by embracing a deep prayer life.

To Understand

It is hard to find heroes today. Sometimes, we have to look to heroes from the past, like Elijah, the zealous prophet. He refuses to accept lame excuses or compromises. In absolute fidelity to the covenant of Yahweh, he repudiates the worship of false gods. Elijah tries to shatter the people's apathy and turn their hearts back to God. "How long will you go limping along with two different opinions? Make up your minds," he demands. But the people do not

36

answer him. Elijah goes to the mountaintop to wait for God's answer. Like Moses on Mt. Sinai, Elijah experiences an earthquake, wind, and fire. However, it is in earnest listening that God is fully heard.

The desire to obey God's will consumes Jesus as it did Moses and Elijah. Jesus takes his faithful disciples up the mountain to hear God's voice as clearly as he does. Both Moses and Elijah appear alongside Jesus. As faithful prophets of God's Word, they understand the price of their calling. When we see Jesus transfigured in splendor, we see a glimpse of his future and, we hope, a forecast of our own. Jesus cautions us not to focus on the glory but on the cross. He doesn't allow us to stay on the mountain; he wants us to go back to the nitty-gritty of the world. When we come down from the clouds, we discover that the path to glory is a difficult journey, one strewn with obstacles that lead to suffering and even death. Back in the everyday world we have trouble comprehending Jesus' words. On the mountaintop God affirmed Jesus' mission, "This is my beloved son. Listen to him." In the humdrum of ordinary life, will we hear Jesus' voice?

To Consider

- Am I able to see Jesus better in mountaintop experiences or in my daily life?
- Do I hear his voice better in victory or defeat?
- When I hear Jesus speak, do I obey his words?

To Pray

Pray Psalm 80: O shepherd God, help me when I am weak and withdrawn from you. Give me new life so I may call upon your name and faithfully follow you.

Third Sunday of Advent (A)

Mt 11:2-11
   Isa 35:1-6,10; Ps 146; Jas 5:7-10

This is the one about whom it is written,
   "See, I am sending my messenger ahead of you,
      who will prepare your way before you." — Mt 11:10

To Note

"Gaudete Sunday" is the traditional name given to the
third Sunday of Advent. The word *gaudete* is Latin for
"rejoice." It is taken from the first word of the opening
antiphon of the Latin introit (*Gaudete in Domino semper*,
"Rejoice in the Lord always"). Rose-colored vestments
may be worn on this day as a sign of joy as our redemption
draws near. An acronym can be made of the word "joy" to
stand for "Jesus, Others, You." When we keep these three
in balance, we spell "joy!"

To Understand

There is something so unexpected and beautiful about
seeing flowers grow in the desert. Flowers are in such stark
contrast to the arid landscape that they take us by surprise.
When we are suffering, our spiritual lives may be as dry as
the desert. We fail to notice that the parched land is in
bloom. When we are frightened or weak, we cannot hear
the strains of the joyful song of God's people. We need the
voice of the prophet saying, "Be strong! Fear not! Here is
your God who comes to save you!" Then the dry riverbeds
overflow with the spring rains. Our eyes are opened to the
beauty around us. Our ears are unstopped and we can hear
the music clearly. Weak limbs are strengthened and we
can walk in freedom. Our hearts are filled with joy.

From his dark prison cell, John the Baptist cannot hear or see Jesus. Questions and uncertainty fill his heart. From our own prisons of doubt and fear we expect to see fire and brimstone fall on our oppressors. "Are you the one, or are we to look for another?" we wonder. Jesus is not the stern judge we had expected. He offers hope to all who suffer hardships: "The blind see, cripples walk, lepers are cured, deaf hear, the dead are raised to life, and the poor have the Gospel of justice preached to them." Liberated by the Gospel, sorrow and mourning flee. We realize that we are the ones who are blind and deaf, sick and lifeless. We do not listen when the Gospel is proclaimed. We are like reeds swaying in the wake of every novel idea. We want a Gospel of prosperity instead of truth and justice. Still, we must be patient with ourselves and one another. We wait in hope, knowing that the fullness of God's reign in our lives is yet to come. The seed planted in the winter must be watered by the spring rain so that it will take root and blossom. John and others have sown the seed. With joy we anticipate the blossoming of Christ in our midst. With him we are confident that we will reap a good harvest.

To Consider

- Do I feel as though I am in prison or in exile? What is keeping me there? How do I imagine it will end?
- How can I liberate those held captive to despair?

To Pray

Light three Advent candles and pray Psalm 146: Lord, you are a faithful God. You secure justice for the oppressed. You raise us up when we are bowed down. You fill us with joy!

Third Sunday of Advent (B)

Jn 1:6-8,19-28
   Isa 61:1-2,10-11; Lk 1; 1 Thess 5:16-24

I am the voice of one crying out in the wilderness,
  "Make straight the way of the Lord." — Jn 1:23

To Note

The coming of Christ brings "joy to the world." Joy is one of the fruits of the Spirit (Gal 5:22). Christian joy surpasses human effort to find pleasure and satisfaction. It is the happiness found in service. Joy comes from a life lived in response to God's love for us. It is a deep abiding joy even in the midst of trials and suffering, a joy that no one can take from us (Jn 16:22). St. Teresa of Avila said that joy is the most infallible sign of the presence of God.

To Understand

John the Baptist announces the glad tidings of the coming of the Lord. He testifies to the truth that shines like a beacon of light in a dark land. John is a powerful witness. He is Spirit-filled, but he is not ego-filled. John is able to give an honest appraisal of himself. He knows that he is not the light; he merely holds the lamp high enough for others to see the coming of the Lord. John is not the Messiah, neither is he Elijah. He is simply a voice crying out to a weary world: "Prepare the way of the Lord!" Joy and praise spring up from the barren ground.

What kind of people should we be while waiting for the Lord? We can follow the example of Mary, who delights in the Lord. Her whole being is joy-filled because God is her savior. Like the prophet Isaiah, Mary announces glad tidings to the dispirited and brokenhearted. God turns the world upside down, exalting the lowly, filling the hungry, and upholding the powerless. God is a gardener who plants justice for the oppressed. God is a faithful lover who has not forgotten the beloved.

Paul is another model for us. Paul could have felt abandoned by God, yet from his dark and lonely prison he still says, "Rejoice!" As we await the Lord's coming to liberate us from our physical, emotional, and mental prisons, we should never stop giving thanks for peace in the midst of trials. We must prepare our hearts with joy. We dare not despise the prophet who calls us to grow and change. We must trust the Spirit who is perfecting us in every way— body, soul, and spirit—to make us a holy and "whole" people ready to greet the Lord when he comes. Then with Isaiah, Paul, John, Mary, and Jesus, we can say: "The Spirit of the Lord is upon *me*. The Lord has anointed *me* to bring good news and healing to the poor and brokenhearted, to release all who are confined in prisons of pain and sin. Through the Spirit, I announce a time of jubilation! I rejoice in God who is my savior!"

To Consider

- What witness can I give concerning Jesus? Is it full of joy or full of doom and gloom?
- What great things has the Lord done for me that I can share with others?

To Pray

Light three Advent candles and pray Luke 1: My soul rejoices in you, my God. My whole being proclaims you as my Savior. Your mercy is upon all generations who give you homage.

Third Sunday of Advent (C)

Lk 3:10-18
  Zeph 3:14-18; Isa 12; Phil 4:4-7

And the crowds asked him, "What then should we do?"
— Lk 3:10

To Note

In his apostolic exhortation *Gaudete in Domino* ("Rejoice in the Lord," May 9, 1975), Pope Paul VI wrote of the immense joy that Christ's birth has brought to all people throughout the ages: "No one is excluded from the joy brought by the Lord. The great joy announced by the Angel on Christmas night is truly for all the people, both for the people of Israel then anxiously awaiting a Savior, and for the numberless people made up of all those who, in time to come, would receive its message and strive to live by it."

To Understand

"Shout for joy, O daughter Zion!" the prophet Zephaniah announces. We are glad because the Lord is in our midst. God is a "mighty savior" who conquers our enemies of "fear" and "defeat." God is a bridegroom who renews us with love. God rejoices with us, singing like pilgrims who have reached their destination after a long journey. "Cry out with gladness!" the prophet Isaiah proclaims. We can be confident and unafraid because God saves us and fills us with courage. Thirsting for grace, we can draw life-giving water from the overflowing fountain of salvation. We drink deeply, and it fills us with joy.

"Rejoice!" Paul says. If we fail to hear him the first time, he repeats his words: "I say it again, rejoice!" Paul's joy is beyond human understanding. How can anyone be joyful when locked in a prison cell with a guard standing over him night and day? Paul says this peace only comes from God, who stands watch over his heart and mind. Paul urges us to present our needs in prayers full of gratitude for the mighty things God has done. By rejoicing always and in *all ways*, we are released from the confines of our prisons and, like Paul, we live in the freedom of Christ.

Still, there must be something more we can do as we await the Lord's coming. John speaks to our practical life situation. "Be generous. Share your food. Share your clothes. Don't browbeat one another. Be honest. Don't blame others for your own misdeeds. Be grateful for what you have." John is filled with anticipation of the one who is to come, yet he humbly acknowledges his own role. John doesn't try to fill the shoes of the Messiah. He knows he is not worthy to loose his master's sandal strap. John baptizes with water as a sign of repentance. Jesus will come with the purifying grace of the Holy Spirit, separating good from evil and purging out all the refuse from our lives.

To Consider

- As a prophet of God, what would I announce? What would I denounce?
- How can I apply John's admonitions to my life?
- How can I fulfill Paul's command to rejoice always?

To Pray

Light three Advent candles and pray Isaiah 12: God, you are my Savior. With joy I proclaim your name and make known your deeds. You are the Holy One in our midst.

Monday of Third Week of Advent

Note: For Masses on December 17-24, see Weekdays of Advent, pages 60-74.

Mt 21:23-27
  Num 24:2-7,15-17; Ps 25

Did the baptism of John come from heaven, or was it of human origin? — *Mt 21:25*

To Note

The Vatican II Dogmatic Constitution on Divine Revelation, *Dei Verbum* (Latin, "Word of God"), declares that "the most intimate truth" which is given to us about God and our salvation "shines forth in Christ, who is himself both the mediator and the sum total of Revelation" (2). God sent Jesus, "the eternal word," to dwell among us and enlighten us "about the inner life of God." Hence, Jesus Christ "speaks the words of God and accomplishes the saving work which the Father gave him to do" (4).

To Understand

The Israelites were on the march to the promised land, but their enemies tried to stop them. The King of Moab wasn't sure he could defeat God's people in battle, but he had another idea. He would pay the renowned prophet Balaam to put a curse on Israel. But God blocked the prophet's way. Only Balaam's jackass could see the divine messenger (a commentary on human efforts to prophecy). When Balaam finally understood, he told the king that he could only speak the words that God put in his mouth. Balaam did not curse Israel. He pronounced a blessing on them, not once but three times. The king flew into a rage, but the divine oracle prevailed: "A star shall come out of Jacob, and a scepter shall rise out of Israel."

Sometimes people can be as stubborn as Balaam's mule. But unlike the mule, they fail to see the works of God even when it is right before their eyes. When Jesus cleanses the temple, making it a place for prayer instead of profit, he is confronted by his enemies who want to know "on whose authority" he has done these things. They see Jesus as an itinerant preacher without credentials. Why should his words have any more significance than anyone else's? Jesus turns the tables on his adversaries and asks them questions, "What was the origin of John's baptism? Human or divine?" Whoops! If they say "divine," Jesus will ask, "Then what's the problem? Why don't you believe in what he does?" If they say "human," the people will be angry because they believe that John is sent by God. They end up admitting they don't know the answer. We're not very different from the people in Jesus' day. We need to admit when we're wrong or when we don't know the answers. We need to ask ourselves the question Jesus asks his critics, "Is this of human or divine origin?"

To Consider

- Do I recognize the authority God gives to the church to teach?
- Do I listen with an open mind to what the church has to say?
- Do I to stand up for the truth on controversial issues?

To Pray

Pray Psalm 25: O Lord, help me to be humble so that you might show me your way. Teach me and guide my path to truth and justice.

Tuesday of Third Week of Advent

Note: For Masses on December 17-24, see Weekdays of Advent, pages 60-74.

Mt 21:28-32
  Zeph 3:1-2,9-13; Ps 34

Truly I tell you, the tax collectors and the prostitutes are going into the kingdom of God ahead of you. — Mt 21:31

To Note

Regarding the formation of conscience, the *Catechism of the Catholic Church* says that people must avail themselves of the means to have a "well-formed conscience" that is "upright and truthful." Moral judgments are formulated "according to reason, in conformity with the true good willed by the wisdom of the Creator. The education of conscience is indispensable for human beings who are subjected to negative influences and tempted by sin to prefer their own judgment and to reject authoritative teachings" (1783).

To Understand

"Woe to those who refuse to hear God's voice or accept correction," the prophet Zephaniah reproaches us. We tremble in our shoes thinking of the times we have been too proud to turn to God and repent. Yet God has no desire to punish us for our rebellious actions. Though God approves the humble and lowly, God doesn't want us to hang our heads in humiliation. God confronts us when we do wrong, but God also rescues us when we are brokenhearted. God wants to purify us so that we may serve one another and dwell in peace. If we contritely call on the name of the Lord, God will hear our pleas for mercy. Then praise will be on our lips instead of lies. We will not blush with shame; we will be radiant with joy.

Jesus challenges his opponents, not to trap them but to persuade them to look at their own actions and change their ways. "What do you think of this case?" Jesus asks the self-righteous who think they're doing God's will but are really only giving lip-service. Jesus' parable hits home with us. We are like the first son in the story when we say that we will do whatever God asks but never put our words in action. The next time we get in trouble we cry, "Oh God, I'll promise you anything," but quickly forget about it when the crisis is over. We are like the second son, too. Often we really don't want to do what God asks. We plant our feet squarely on the ground and stubbornly refuse. Later, we might think it over and regret our words. We may not like it better, but we do what God wants. Jesus asks us to look at our lives and decide what kind of sons or daughters we want to be. Do we want to brag to others about the wonderful things we plan to do for God and never do them? Or do we admit that we are weak "sinners" and reform our lives?

To Consider:

· Am I more like the son who says yes but really means no?
· Am I like the son who says no but struggles to say yes?
· When do I see examples of each in myself?

To Pray

Pray Psalm 34: Lord, help me to turn to you. Remove my shame when I call out in distress. Hear my prayer so that I can be filled with joy.

Wednesday of Third Week of Advent

Note: For Masses on December 17-24, see Weekdays of Advent, pages 60-74.

Lk 7:18-23
  Isa 45:6-8,18,21-25; Ps 85

And blessed is anyone who takes no offense at me. — Lk 7:23

To Note

The U.S. Bishops' statement on the environment declares: "It is to the Creator of the universe, then, that we are accountable for what we do or fail to do to preserve and care for the earth and all its creatures." In our role as God's stewards and co-creators, "fullness of life comes from living responsibly with God's creation." The bishops say further, "We must care for all God's creatures, especially the most vulnerable. How, then, can we protect endangered species and at the same time be callous to the unborn, the elderly or disabled persons?" (*Renewing the Earth*, 1991, U.S. Catholic Conference).

To Understand

The unthinkable happens! The Holy City is invaded, the walls breached and torn down, the beautiful temple burned and desecrated. Suffering is everywhere, dead bodies strewn about, homes and fields scorched and smoldering. Those who survive are slaves in chains, dragged off to exile. Hopelessness and despair fill the air as much as the foul stench of warfare. "Where is God in all this?" the people cry out in anguish. The prophet Isaiah speaks: "Shower, O heavens, from above, and let the skies rain down righteousness; let the earth open, that salvation may

48

bud forth and justice spring up." God swears an unalterable decree. "Turn to me and be safe, all you ends of the earth," says the Lord, "for I am God; there is no other." God has spoken and it will be so.

John the Baptist proclaims Jesus as the great prophet, the one who comes from God to lead the people to salvation, truth, and justice. But when we are held captive to suffering—death of a loved one, divorce, cancer, Alzheimer's, AIDS, or other catastrophic event—it is hard to see God in it. Are diseases really cured? Can sense be made out of the death of an innocent child? Is there any meaning to be found in mindless destruction, an earthquake, or a tornado? Is God punishing us for our sins? Whom can we trust? Like John the Baptist, we must look to Jesus in times of trial. In Jesus' dying and rising we discover that a broken body is not a sign of God's punishment. God was not absent at the cross. Neither was God missing in Auschwitz, Rwanda, nor Oklahoma City. The choice between good and evil is one we all must make, whether to destroy or heal the world. When we discover God's truth, then peace and justice will appear on the earth.

To Consider

- Do I pray for the healing of the world from natural and human destruction?
- What is my contribution toward the efforts of peace, justice, and care for the environment?
- What is one thing I can do during Advent?

To Pray

Pray Psalm 85: Lord help me to hear what you proclaim. Help me to walk the way of justice, in the footsteps of your Son.

Thursday of Third Week of Advent

Note: For Masses on December 17-24, see Weekdays of Advent, pages 60-74.

Lk 7:24-30
  Isa 54:1-10; Ps 30

Jesus began to speak to the crowds about John: "What did you go out into the wilderness to look at? A reed shaken by the wind?" — Lk 7:24

To Note

While we can never fathom the mystery of suffering, we must correct our misconception about God's role in our pain. A distorted view of God can harm our relationship with God and stifle our prayer life. St. Francis de Sales, Doctor of the Church, stressed the possibility of sanctity in everyday trials: "The same everlasting Father who cares for you today will take care of you tomorrow and every day. Either he will shield you from suffering, or he will give you unfailing strength to bear it. Be at peace then and put aside all anxious thoughts and imaginations."

To Understand

The people in exile felt as barren as a childless woman, as cast off as a wife abandoned by her husband. At nightfall, tears soaked their pillows. Their perception of a loving, compassionate God was obscured by the darkness in their lives. Yahweh was seen as a wrathful God who punished them unmercifully for their sins. Had God disavowed the covenant and forsaken them? Isaiah says that their idea of God is too small. God is their creator, their redeemer, their lover who has espoused them in faithfulness. Though dispossessed from their land in disgrace, they will not be put to shame. God's covenant of peace shall never be shaken.

The people in Jesus' day were wandering aimlessly, looking for some meaning in their lives. In the past, they heard the voice of God speaking to them in the desert. Now they go out there again to see if God will speak to them anew. In the wilderness they find a wild-eyed prophet who speaks relentlessly about the need to change their lives. God must not be blamed for their desperate state. They must take responsibility for their own failings. Jesus challenges us. "Why did you go out to the desert? Certainly not to see someone rich and powerful, dressed in fine clothes. You can find people like that in the royal palaces if that's what you want to see." Jesus asks us to think again, "What did you go out to see? A prophet? Yes, and more than a prophet, a messenger who prepares the way for the coming of God." Jesus asks us to examine our motives. What do we want? What are we looking for in life? Have we heard John's message and reformed our lives? Or do we turn our backs on God's gift of Jesus and defeat the divine plan to save us from our own sinfulness?

To Consider

- Do I blame God when I face trials and troubles?
- Do I take responsibility for my own actions?
- Am I listening to the messengers God sends this Advent? What am I doing about it?

To Pray

Pray Psalm 30: Lord, I want to be one of your faithful ones. I want to praise you for changing my tears to joy. You have transformed my mourning into dancing.

Friday of Third Week of Advent

Note: For Masses on December 17-24, see Weekdays of Advent, pages 60-74.

Jn 5:33-36
   Isa 56:1-3,6-8; Ps 67

The works that the Father has given me to complete, the very works that I am doing, testify on my behalf that the Father has sent me. — Jn 5:36

To Note

The eight-day Jewish feast of Hanukkah falls during the same season as Christmas. This festival commemorates the rededication of the temple after it had been desecrated by the Syrians, who had made it a shrine to the pagan god Zeus. Under the leadership of the Maccabees, the Judeans defeated the might of Syria and reclaimed the temple. Though they only had enough oil to relight the temple lamps for one day, miraculously it lasted for eight days (1 Macc 4:36-59). Hanukkah and Christmas share the common themes of light and peace.

To Understand

The prophet Isaiah says that those who obey God's words will be blessed for heeding them. That must be us, right, God? We are the righteous ones. All those other people—the ones who don't go to church, especially my church—they must be sinners. And what about those foreigners whose beliefs are different than ours? How can we worship with them? And those people whose lifestyles are unacceptable to us. Aren't they responsible for all the problems in society today? The prophet stops us short.

52

"Let no one say, 'The Lord will exclude me.'" God has no favorites. Anyone who acts with faith and justice is acceptable to God. All the barriers we arbitrarily construct—religion, race, gender, culture, nationality, economic or social class—are knocked down by God. All people are welcome in God's house of prayer.

John the Baptist echoes the words of the prophet Isaiah: "Observe what is right, do what is just; for my salvation is about to come, my justice, about to be revealed." John points the way to Jesus, who is the fullness of God's revelation. John is a "voice" crying out to be heard by all, but Jesus is the living "word" of God. John is a "lamp" illuminating the pathway to Jesus, but Jesus is the "light" of the world, set aflame for all eternity. John's witness to Jesus is powerful, but Jesus' own testimony is far greater. The works that he performs bear an incredible witness that God has sent him. Jesus was sent to his own people, yet they fail to come to him for the very life they seek. Because they refuse to believe in him, Jesus will gather others. The outcast, lost, rejected, and marginalized will all be welcome at God's banquet table.

To Consider

- Do I testify to the power of Jesus in my life?
- Do I fail to recognize his words and works in the lives of people who are different than myself?
- How can I help make my community a house of prayer for all people?

To Pray

Pray Psalm 67: Have pity on us, God, and bless all your people. Let your light shine upon us. Make your way to salvation known upon the earth, among all the nations.

Fourth Sunday of Advent (A)

Mt 1:18-24
  Isa 7:10-14; Ps 24; Rom 1:1-7

Joseph, son of David, do not be afraid to take Mary as your wife, for the child conceived in her is from the Holy Spirit.
— *Mt 1:20*

To Note

We honor Mary as the virgin Mother of Jesus, but we must also uphold Joseph as a role model of a faithful husband and father. If we are concerned about the weakening of traditional roles of women as wives and mothers, we must also be concerned about male role models in families. The absence of men who are committed to their wives and children is cited as a major factor in today's sociological problems: single-parent households, poverty, domestic violence, adolescent pregnancy, and criminal behavior of youth. Joseph provides a standard for men, supportive during pregnancy and responsible providers and protectors of the family.

To Understand

When someone is weak and defenseless, that person may be tempted to join forces with the powers of the world, even if it is the enemy. King Ahaz was in such a position. The prophet Isaiah tells the king not to trust such a partnership but to have confidence that God will save him. Ahaz would rather enlist the aid of his enemy than put his trust in God.

Isaiah tells the king that if it is too hard to have faith in God's deliverance, he should ask God for a sign. Ahaz is too proud to do that, so he refuses. God is not outwitted by the king's self-deception. God gives Ahaz a sign, not lightning and thunder but a child born to a young woman. Before the child reaches maturity, the king's enemies will be overcome. The sign contains a promise that is more than Ahaz can imagine. It points to one who saves us from all that threatens us.

After centuries of waiting, the sign is fulfilled, but not in the way anyone could envision. The child is not born to the rich and powerful but to an insignificant young virgin espoused to an ordinary carpenter. Joseph has hopes and dreams for his future with Mary. When he hears that she is pregnant, he is in a dilemma. What will people say? Will they understand? Joseph can't understand it himself. Mary will surely be stoned to death as an adulteress. Joseph can't bear to think of that. Should he get rid of her, and the child too? But God's messenger tells Joseph, "Don't be afraid." The child is conceived by the Holy Spirit and is to be named *Emmanuel*, meaning "God is with us." Like Joseph, no matter how difficult our struggles may be, we need to trust that God is with us!

To Consider

- In what ways is Joseph a model for today?
- Is he an example for my own life?
- In times of trouble, do I trust that God is with me despite my perplexity?

To Pray

Light four Advent candles and pray Psalm 24: Lord, you are the king of glory. Enter my life so I may stand chaste and virtuous before you, ready to do your will.

Fourth Sunday of Advent (B)

Lk 1:26-38
   2 Sam 7:1-5,8-11,16; Ps 89; Rom 16:25-27

Then Mary said, "Here am I, the servant of the Lord; let it be with me according to your word." — Lk 1:38

To Note

"Yeshu'a," the Aramaic version of the Hebrew name "Yehoshu'a," or "Joshua," means "Yahweh is salvation." When the Gospels were written in Greek, "Yeshu'a" became "Iesous," pronounced "yeh-SOOS." St. Jerome translated the Bible into Latin in the fourth century (the Vulgate version), and "Iesous" became "Iesus," pronounced "YAY-soos." In the fourteenth century, German monks elongated the "I" into a "J" and pronounced our Lord's name, "Yay-zoos." With the Norman Conquest of England, the French pronunciation of "J" ("zh") was introduced. When King James had the bible translated into English in 1611, the Latin "Jesus" was carried over and eventually evolved into the modern English "Jee-zus."

To Understand

The stronghold of Zion is captured, and David sets up his throne in Jerusalem, to be known forever as the "City of David." He finally has time to rest from his enemies. He has been too busy building his own kingdom to be worried about God's domain; now he notices the splendid house he lives in while a simple tent serves as the dwelling place of the ark of the Lord. David summons the prophet Nathan and tells him of his plans to build a sumptuous house for the Lord. But God appears to Nathan and tells him that David has it all backward. David was a simple shepherd boy when God appointed him commander of Israel. God made David as famous as all the great ones of the earth. God has always been with David, destroying his enemies before him. Now that Israel is established as a people, God will build a house for David, not one of cedar or bricks and mortar but a kingdom that will endure forever.

This mystery, hidden throughout the ages, is manifested in Jesus. By command of the eternal God, the angel Gabriel is sent to the insignificant town of Nazareth to a humble woman named Mary. God's messenger greets Mary with a joyful salutation: "Rejoice, O highly favored daughter! The Lord is with you!" Mary is blessed among all women on earth for she will conceive and bear a son whose name is Jesus, meaning "savior." Mary's child is the "Son of the Most High," who is given the throne of David. His reign will be without end. Mary is mystified at the promise, but nothing is impossible with God. Just as the divine presence filled the temple of Jerusalem, the Holy Spirit overshadows Mary, the holy temple of the Lord. The child conceived in her womb is the "Son of God," who will save the people from their sins. God's spirit fills us, too. With Mary, each of us must say, "I am your servant. Do with me as you will."

To Consider

- Do I understand Mary as a model for discipleship?
- How has she inspired my own life of service?
- In what area of my life do I need to submit to God's will?

To Pray

Light four Advent candles and pray Psalm 89: Lord, I will sing of your goodness forever. You are my God, my Rock, my Savior.

Fourth Sunday of Advent (C)

Lk 1:39-45
  Mic 5:1-4; Ps 80; Heb 10:5-10

Blessed are you among women, and blessed is the fruit of your womb. — Lk 1:42

To Note

In the Bible, a name represents the reality and presence of that person. The name of Jesus carries the power and authority of God, who saves. When Jesus' name is invoked in prayer, he is present to help us. Christians are baptized in his name. We bow our heads and bend our knees at the name of Jesus. His name should always be spoken with reverence, not to curse or swear. Through Jesus' death and resurrection, we are sent in the power of Jesus' name to act by his authority. The name of Jesus should be used to confront the powers of evil and bring peace and justice to the world.

To Understand

Like the prophets of old, Jesus announces, "Here I am! I come to do your will!" Jesus enters the world with one purpose: to accomplish God's saving will. His name signifies his work: "Yahweh saves." God's ancient covenant is fulfilled in Jesus' new covenant. Burnt sacrifices, holocausts, and sin offerings cannot compare to Jesus' perfect offering of his body and blood for the sins of the world. The time of fulfillment is at hand. The ruler of God's people is to be born in Bethlehem, David's birthplace. This little town, situated near the great city of Jerusalem, was too small to draw the attention of Judah's kings. But in contrast to their weak leadership, a mighty king will emerge as the defender of God's people. Though Israel and Judah will go into captivity and the kingship will die, a new king like David will restore the people once more. As David shepherded his flock, Jesus will guide the people by the Lord's own strength. They will no longer be "fenced in" as a captive people. Jesus will lead the flock to freedom. The greatness of his reign of peace will reach the ends of the earth.

When Mary conceives the savior child, she cannot keep this good news to herself. In haste, she goes to her cousin Elizabeth in the hill country in Judah. Incredibly, Elizabeth, who is in her advanced years, is also pregnant. Her child will be called John. He is "the Baptist," who will announce the coming of the Messiah of God. With Mary's greeting, the child leaps for joy in Elizabeth's womb, just as David danced before the ark of the Lord when it was brought into Jerusalem. David was awed by the divine presence, and Elizabeth is amazed to be in the presence of the ark of the new covenant, Mary, the mother of the Lord. Filled with God's Spirit, Elizabeth's joyful cry of exultation becomes our prayer: "Blessed are you among women, and blessed is the fruit of your womb."

To Consider

- Am I aware of the Lord's presence in the Eucharist?
- Do I recognize his presence in my life and in others' lives?
- Have I shared him with others this Advent?

To Pray

Light four Advent candles and pray Psalm 80: Lord, help us to turn to you so we might call upon your name to be saved. Fill us with new life as Mary was filled with Jesus.

Weekday of Advent (December 17)

Note: The following Scriptures are used in the Mass on the day assigned, with the exception of Sunday.

Mt 1:1-17
   Gen 49:2,8-10; Ps 72

An account of the genealogy of Jesus the Messiah, the son of David, the son of Abraham. — Mt 1:1

To Note

Since the eighth century, the last seven days of Advent preceding Christmas Eve have been set aside to reflect on the meaning of Christmas: the salvation that Jesus Christ brings. The Gospel antiphons for Mass and Evening Prayer of these days are known as the "O Antiphons" (Greek, "answering voice"). The O Antiphons, sung before and after the Magnificat, are so named because each antiphon begins with the exclamation "O." These antiphons name the Christ who comes into the world and into our hearts. The first antiphon is "O Wisdom." Christ is the wisdom of God, who possesses the strength, understanding, and guidance for which we yearn (Wis 7:7,15; 1 Cor 1:20-25).

To Understand

Jacob's name was changed by the angel of God to "Israel." His twelve sons are the foundation stones of the nation of Israel. When Jacob was dying, he called his twelve sons together and blessed them. Judah, the fourth son, is given a pledge of enduring kingship. Judah is a "lion's cub," appointed to rule with wisdom and authority. From his line will come David, king of Israel. The scepter shall never depart from Judah's tribe until it can be presented to the one to whom it rightfully belongs. The lion of Judah will roar when God's kingdom is established through Jesus Christ.

Matthew begins his Gospel with a genealogy to show that Jesus is the fulfillment of God's promises to Israel. Jesus is the faithful son of Abraham, through whom all nations are blessed. Matthew traces Jesus' lineage from the glorious days of King David to the agonizing days of the Babylonian captivity. Through Joseph, Jesus is the descendant of David to whom God promised a permanent throne. Jesus is "the Christ" (Greek: *Christos*), the expected "Messiah" (Hebrew: *Mâshiah*), the "anointed one" of God. In Jesus' virgin birth through Mary, he is the Son of God, the messianic king endowed with power to save the people from their sins. Among Jesus' ancestors are listed four non-Jewish women whose children are conceived through unconventional relationships. Jesus comes for the salvation of all people regardless of status, gender, nationality, or race. Jesus is God's wisdom personified, who leads us to all truth.

To Consider

- Do I patiently seek God's wisdom even when I don't understand events in my life?
- What does my family tree tell me about myself?
- Do I see myself as adopted into God's family?

To Pray

Pray O Antiphon: O Wisdom, O Holy Word of God, you come to govern the universe with your strong yet gentle care. O come, and teach us the way of truth.

Weekday of Advent (December 18)

Note: The following Scriptures are used in the Mass on the day assigned, with the exception of Sunday.

Mt 1:18-24
  Jer 23:5-8; Ps 72

She will bear a son, and you are to name him Jesus, for he will save his people from their sins. — Mt 1:21

To Note:

"O Adonai" is the second O Antiphon. "Adonai" is the Hebrew plural for "my Lord" (Greek: *Kyrios*). During the post-exilic period, "Adonai" was used by Jews as a title for God out of reverence for the unspeakable name "Yahweh." The word "Jehovah" found in some texts is an artificial form for the name of God. Scribes inserted the vowels of "Adonai," a-o-a, between the four consonants of "Yahweh," Y-H-W-H (Greek: *tetragrammaton*, "four letters"), creating the incorrect hybrid word "YaHoWaH" or "Jehovah." Jesus is "Lord" through his resurrection from the dead (Rom 4:24). In his coming in glory, Jesus our Lord will establish God's reign (Rev 11:15).

To Understand

"The days are coming!" Jeremiah utters a cry of joy in anticipation of God's redemption of Israel. The nation has been invaded and devastated. The family tree of David has been cut to its roots. The people no longer hope that God's promise of an everlasting kingdom will be realized. But Jeremiah says, "Look! There is life in the old tree yet!" A tiny green shoot remains on the barren tree, a fragile sign of future restoration. The people must not live in the past, remembering how God had delivered their ancestors from slavery in Egypt. They can boast, "The Lord has brought *us* out of bondage."

"Now this is how it happened," Matthew tells us how we received salvation. That green shoot on Jesse's tree is Jesus our Lord. Mary can hardly believe that she is so privileged. She is to be the mother of the promised Messiah of God, the one who will set his people free. Joseph finds it hard to believe that he will participate in so great an event. Mary is blessed and grace-filled, but Joseph is fearful. "Do not be afraid!" the angel tells Joseph, who is to name the child "Jesus," "Savior," because he will liberate his people from their sins! Jesus is Emmanuel, "God is with us!" Joseph need not fear if God is with him, and he wastes no time obeying the message. Joseph takes Mary into his home and lives chastely with her. When the time comes to fulfill all that has been announced by the prophets, Mary bears Jesus, the incarnate God who dwells among the people. At the end of Matthew's Gospel, Jesus says: "Remember, I am with you always, to the end of the age."

To Consider

- When there are trials and I am discouraged, do I turn to Jesus as lord of my life?
- Is Jesus my Lord in the good times as well?
- What areas of my life do I need to surrender to his lordship?

To Pray

Pray O Antiphon: O Adonai, sacred Lord of Israel who shows yourself to us as you did to Moses in the burning bush, stretch out your hand to set your people free once more.

Weekday of Advent (December 19)

Note: The following Scriptures are used in the Mass on the day assigned, with the exception of Sunday.

Lk 1:5-25
  Judg 13:2-7,24-25; Ps 71

Do not be afraid, Zechariah, for your prayer has been heard. Your wife Elizabeth will bear you a son, and you will name him John. — Lk 1:13

To Note

"Root of Jesse" is the third O Antiphon. Jesse of Bethlehem was the father of David, Israel's greatest king. After the Babylonian exile, only a stump of the mighty tree of David remained. The prophet Isaiah announced that the root of Jesse would blossom as a sign to draw all people from the "four corners of the earth" (Isa 11:10-12). Through Joseph, Jesus is born in David's royal line. Jesus flowers as the fulfillment of the people's hopes. On the wood of the cross, Jesus shows us God's love by drawing all people to himself (Jn 12:32).

To Understand

In the Bible, women are often depicted as barren to show God's power to bring fruitfulness in our lives. Manoah and her husband Zorah were peasants from the tribe of Dan. Like other women in the Bible—Sarah, Rebecca, Rachel and Hannah—Manoah is childless. Then the impossible happens. An angel of the Lord announces, "Though you are barren, you will conceive and bear a son." Manoah begs the Lord to teach her what she must do and she is given some sound prenatal instructions: "Be careful to take no wine or strong drink and to eat nothing unclean." The child that Manoah bears is Samson, the pride of the Israelites, a larger-than-life hero. Samson is consecrated to the Lord, "set apart" (Hebrew: *nezir*) through his "Nazirite" vow. During the period of dedication, no liquor is drunk, and his hair and beard are not cut as a sign of devotion to Yahweh. As "judge" of Israel, the spirit of the Lord is upon Samson to enable him to accomplish marvelous military feats. His great strength is a testimony to the saving power of God.

Like many of her ancestors, Elizabeth is also barren. She and her husband, Zechariah, are a bit more upscale than Samson's folks. Elizabeth is a descendant of the priest Aaron, and Zechariah is a member of the priestly class. One day, as Zechariah burns incense in the temple, the divine messenger Gabriel appears to him and announces the birth of a son. Like Samson, this child is divinely chosen. He too will drink no strong drink and will be filled by the spirit from his mother's womb. Zechariah cannot believe what he hears, so, as a sign, he will be mute until the birth of his son. Paradoxically, the child will be John the Baptist, a loud "voice" who heralds the coming of the Lord.

To Consider

- Do I appreciate the sacredness of human life?
- In what ways have I been called and consecrated by God?
- How am I fulfilling my mission?

To Pray

Pray O Antiphon: O flower of Jesse's stem, you have been raised up as a sign for all peoples. Kings and nations bow down to worship you. Come in haste to deliver us.

Weekday of Advent (December 20)

Note: The following Scriptures are used in the Mass on the day assigned, with the exception of Sunday.

Lk 1:26-38
  Isa 7:10-14; Ps 24

He will be great, and will be called the Son of the Most High, and the Lord God will give to him the throne of his ancestor David. — Lk 1:32

To Note

The fourth O Antiphon is "Key of David." In the story of Adam and Eve, the couple disobeys God, and they are expelled from the garden of Eden. An angel of the Lord guards the gateway to paradise with a flaming sword (Gen 3:22-24). The image is one of separation from God, the human race held captive to sin and ignorance. When we were powerless to reconcile ourselves to God, God promised a redeemer, the offspring of the New Eve, who will crush the head of sin and death (Gen 3:15). Jesus is the promised one who is given "the key of the house of David" (Isa 22:22). Jesus reopens the gates of heaven and restores us to life eternal. What he has opened, none shall shut.

To Understand

It is a time of threat and turmoil for the people of God. The once-powerful kingdom of David is on the verge of defeat. The northern kingdom of Israel has joined forces with Syria against the southern kingdom of Judah. Though King Ahaz is a legitimate king on David's throne, he is weak and worldly. Ahaz is more concerned about his own position than about guarding the security of the nation. He makes up his mind to form an alliance with the Assyrians. Why not strike a deal and protect yourself and the throne in the bargain? God has a better offer: "Trust me!" The king is not so sure he can trust anyone but himself. The prophet Isaiah urges Ahaz, "Ask God for a sign. Let it be as deep as the earth or as high as the sky. Just ask." Despite the king's stubbornness, God gives a sign. A child shall be born and his name shall be Emmanuel, meaning "God is with us!"

"Rejoice, O highly favored daughter," the angel Gabriel announces to Mary. "The Lord is with you!" Mary is deeply troubled. She knows that God is with her, but she is not prepared for the way God chooses to come to her. The power of the Most High God overshadows her fears. Mary's offspring is the rightful heir to the throne of David, and his rule shall be without end. He is called Jesus, the one who holds the key to the salvation of the people. "How can this be?" the young woman asks. God gives a sign to Mary that cannot be denied. Though it seems impossible, her aged cousin Elizabeth has also conceived a son. Mary humbly submits to God's will. "I am the servant of the Lord. Let it be done to me as you say."

To Consider

- Do I refuse to trust God when I am troubled?
- What do I need to submit to God's will today?
- What "signs" have I received that God is with me?

To Pray

Pray O Antiphon: O Key of David, O royal scepter of Israel, come break down the prison walls and lead forth all those held captive to sin. Enlighten all who sit in darkness in the shadow of death.

Weekday of Advent (December 21)

Note: The following Scriptures are used in the Mass on the day assigned, with the exception of Sunday.

Lk 1:39-45
  Song 2:8-14 or Zeph 3:14-18; Ps 33

*And blessed is she who believed that there would be a fulfill-
ment of what was spoken to her by the Lord. — Lk 1:45*

To Note

"O Dayspring" is the fifth O Antiphon. Advent has its roots in nature's cycle of the winter solstice, when the sun is farthest south of the equator, when darkness is longest and light is shortest. In 274, the Roman Emperor Aurelian declared December 25 the "Feast of the Invincible Sun," marking the triumph of day over night. By 336, the Roman Christians kept their own festival on December 25 in honor of Christ's birth, perhaps to rally against the pagan festival, which honored the god Saturn. Today, our faith affirms that Christ is the "sun of righteousness [who] will rise with healing in its wings" (Mal 4:2) to rescue us from the darkness and bring us into the light of his presence.

To Understand

"Shout for joy, O daughter Zion! Sing joyfully, O Israel!" the prophet Zephaniah exults. Though few in number, the survivors of the exile are summoned to put away fear; God is a mighty savior in their midst. The prophet's images of God are astounding! God sings and dances as one rejoices at a festival. God is a lover, racing toward the beloved over the hills and mountains that have separated them. God renews the worn-out captives with love: "My beautiful

68

one, come! For see, the winter is past, the rains are over and gone. The flowers appear on the earth." God's beloved appears like a dove hiding in the clefts of the rock. She answers, "I come!"

Mary is faithful Zion, the New Eve, obedient to God's call to be mother of the Messiah. She sets out in haste, striding across the hill country to the home of her cousin Elizabeth, who, though barren, has conceived a child in her old age. Mary calls a greeting, and the baby in her cousin's womb leaps for joy. Elizabeth is filled with the Holy Spirit at the sound of Mary's voice. The Lord's promise to Elizabeth and her son is exceedingly great. Greater still is the promise to Mary and her child. "Blessed are you among women, and blessed is the fruit of your womb!" Elizabeth stands awestruck in the presence of the Lord. "Who am I that the mother of my Lord comes to me?" Elizabeth pronounces a blessing on Mary, "Blessed is she who trusted that the Lord's words to her would be fulfilled." The voice of the church, the new Israel, continues to resound: "Hail Mary! Fill our barren lives with the joy of the Lord. Revive our hope in the coming of the savior who sets us free from all that holds us captive to darkness."

To Consider

- How has sadness or depression affected my life this Advent?
- In what ways can I find joy and hope?
- Can I be a source of light to others who sit in darkness?

To Pray

Pray O Antiphon: O Radiant Dawn, Christ our light, eternal son of justice, come enlighten this world darkened by sin. Awaken a ray of hope in the gray winter of our hearts.

Weekday of Advent (December 22)

Note: The following Scriptures are used in the Mass on the day assigned, with the exception of Sunday.

Lk 1:46-56
  1 Sam 1:24-28; 1 Sam 2

For he has looked with favor on the lowliness of his servant.
  Surely, from now on all generations will call me blessed.
— *Lk 1:48*

To Note

The sixth O Antiphon is "O King of the Nations." Ancient kings were identified with the dying and rising god of the fertility festival of the New Year and served as an intermediary between gods and the people. As judge, the king's counsel was available to his subjects. In the New Testament, the true kingship of Jesus is presented. In the palm procession, the people acclaim him as a king like David, who would restore the monarchy. Though Jesus fled from such acclamation (Jn 6:15), he accepts the title "King of the Jews" from Pilate, who places it as an inscription on the cross (Mk 15:2,26). Jesus is a humble king who intercedes on behalf of his people, judges them with mercy, and establishes God's kingdom of peace and justice for all peoples.

To Understand

Like so many women in the Bible, Hannah is barren. In prayer and tears she beseeches the Lord to make her fruitful. When at last she conceives and bears a son, Samuel, she fulfills her pledge to dedicate him to God's service. In gratitude to God, she presents the child to Eli,

70

priest of the temple in Shiloh. As long as Samuel lives, he serves the people as judge, priest, and prophet. When he dies, "all Israel assembled and mourned him."

Like Hannah, Mary utters thanksgiving for the good things the Lord has done for her. Her Magnificat proclaims the greatness of God. She recognizes her lowly role as God's servant whose lofty status comes from the merciful God who is her savior. She pronounces God's judgment on those who have oppressed the poor and ignored their needs. Those who are hungry for God are filled with good things. Those who are self-satisfied and have no room for God's blessings are left empty-handed and barren. Mary is servant Israel, whom God rewards by fulfilling the promises made to Abraham. Through her child, all generations sing praise for the mighty things God has done for, with, and through Mary.

We can choose to be like Hannah and Mary. We can be grateful for God's gifts, or we can wither up with bitterness. We can offer God thankful praise or complain about how we have been victimized. We can serve the poor and hungry or ignore their plight. Hannah and Mary respond with generosity and joy. Do we?

To Consider

- Do I recognize God's gifts in my life?
- How has God lifted my spirit when I felt cast down?
- What meaing does "kingship" have today?

To Pray

Pray O Antiphon: O King of every human heart, you are the cornerstone joining heaven and earth, the mighty arch which makes us one. O come and save your people.

Weekday of Advent (December 23)

Note: The following Scriptures are used in the Mass on the day assigned, with the exception of Sunday.

Lk 1:57-66
 Mal 3:1-4,23-24; Ps 25

"What then will this child become?" For, indeed, the hand of the Lord was with him. — Lk 1:66

To Note

"O Emmanuel" is the seventh and last O Antiphon. "Emmanuel" is the Greek form of the Hebrew "Immanuel," a compound name of the words *immanu*, meaning "with us," and *El*, meaning "God." The name "Emmanuel" is a guarantee of God's presence and provision throughout our life and the destiny of life's pilgrimage. The title "Emmanuel" is given to Jesus, who fulfills the covenant promise given to Moses: "I will be with you" (Ex 3:12). Before his ascension into heaven, Jesus assured his disciples: "I am with you always, to the end of the age" (Mt 28:20).

To Understand

Jesus breaks into our lives when we least expect him. Jesus comes to us in many ways. He comes when we pray with the community or when we seek his presence alone. He comes as our savior to comfort us in times of crisis. He comes as our brother to share our joy or appease the strife in our families. He comes as a friend to challenge us at the turning points in life's journey. He comes as our ruler and lord, asking obedience when the path is difficult. At times, we cannot bear his presence; it is too overwhelming, too demanding. We are afraid of his judgment. But Jesus does not come to condemn us. He is like a refiner, purifying us as precious gold and silver in the fire of his love. Though it is painful to be tested, when we endure the trial, we are pleasing to God, worthy to be called sons and daughters. Jesus is Emmanuel, the one who reveals the love, mercy, and friendship of God.

John's coming was expected. Elizabeth's time to bear a child had arrived. Her relatives and friends rejoice with her at the birth of a son. "Will you call him Zechariah after his father?" they ask. "His name is John," Elizabeth declares in obedience to the messenger of God. "No one in your family has that name," the people protest. Zechariah takes a writing slate and scribbles the words, "His name is to be John." The people are amazed when Zechariah begins to speak and sing the praises of God! They recognize God's presence in these events and ask, "What will this child be? Surely the hand of the Lord is upon him." John is the messenger who announces the coming of God among us: "Make ready the way of the Lord! Clear his path for he comes to save us!"

To Consider

· Is Jesus "Emmanuel" in my life?
· When has he made his presence known?
· Have I told others that he is with us?

To Pray

Pray O Antiphon: O Emmanuel, you are my king and judge, ruler and savior. Be with me in all the places on my journey. O desire of all peoples, come save us.

73

Weekday of Advent (December 24) — Morning Mass

Note: The following Scriptures are used in the Mass on the day assigned, with the exception of Sunday.

Lk 1:67-79
    2 Sam 7:1-5,8-11,16; Ps 89

Blessed be the Lord God of Israel,
* for he has looked favorably on his people*
*   and redeemed them. — Lk 1:68*

To Note

The Advent custom of Las Posadas is popular among the Spanish-speaking world and others. The word *posada* means "shelter" or "inn." The custom reenacts Mary and Joseph's search for lodging on their journey to Bethlehem. Las Posadas lasts nine days (December 16-24) to represent the nine months of Mary's pregnancy. The participants travel from house to house singing a traditional hymn of those who seek lodging and of innkeepers who refuse them. Though hospitality is an important virtue in the Middle East, the procession depicts Luke's saying that there was no room in the place where travelers lodged (Lk 2:7). It prefigures Christ's rejection by those whom he had come to save (Jn 1:11).

To Understand

How would we build a house for the Lord? We can imagine what we would do if we were involved in a parish renovation. How would the church be constructed? Where would the altar be placed? What size would the ambo be? How would the assembly be seated? What would the baptismal font look like? Our creativity could run wild. King David had such a proposition in mind. He was settled in a palace when he noticed that the ark of the covenant resided in a tent! God had bigger plans—not for a grand temple; that will be left to another king. God's plans are for David himself. The shepherd-warrior-king will be given a throne and a kingdom that will outlast all human structures.

Zechariah had been silenced for his unbelief in God's promise of a son. Now his tongue is loosened when the child is born. Zechariah praises God for visiting the people with strength and saving power. The oath that was sworn to Abraham and David has been fulfilled. Elizabeth and Zechariah's child is the "prophet of the Most High" who will prepare the pathway for the coming of the one who will visit them with mercy.

How would we build a house for the Lord? Perhaps we need to be reminded of David and allow God to reconstruct us first. Then we will be a suitable dwelling place for God's son. When we present ourselves at the altar, the place of worship will be transformed by the Lord's presence in us.

To Consider

Take a few moments in this busy day to become aware of God's presence. Reflect on how you have prepared yourself for the coming of the Lord.

To Pray

Pray Psalm 89: Lord, you have established your covenant forever, your throne for all generations. I will sing praises to your faithfulness toward your servants.

Immaculate Conception (December 8)

Lk 1:26-38
    Gen 3:9-15,20; Ps 98; Eph 1:3-6,11-12

Greetings, favored one! The Lord is with you. — Lk 1:28

To Note

The dogma of the Immaculate Conception of Mary was
defined by Pope Pius IX, December 8, 1854. The term
"immaculate" refers to Mary being sinless, "full of grace,"
from the moment of her conception in her mother's womb.
Mary was "favored" by God, as proclaimed in the angelic
salutation to Mary at Jesus' divine conception. Through
the grace of God and the merits of Jesus Christ, her soul
was infused with sanctifying grace. This feast demon-
strates Jesus' redemptive power prior to any human merit
or work. Mary is the patron of the United States under the
title "Immaculate Conception," the name she revealed to
St. Bernadette of Lourdes.

To Understand

After centuries of longing for the Messiah, a divine messenger is sent to proclaim the most glorious event the world
has ever known. The woman's name is Mary, Miriam, "the
exalted one" in God's eyes. The angel declares, "Rejoice
Mary! You have found favor with God! You are full of
grace! You are blessed among all women!" Mary ponders
the joyful salutation. Why does she alone deserve this
honor? Is there a price to pay for so great a privilege? "Do
not be afraid, Mary." God's messenger tells her the incredible reason God has blessed her. Mary shall conceive and
bear a son. Her child shall be called Jesus, meaning "Yahweh saves." Her son is the savior of all people. Mary is

incredulous. How can this be? She is unmarried, a virgin. The angel's answer is even more mysterious. Just as God's spirit overshadowed the holy temple with power, the Spirit of God will come upon her. Mary is the dwelling place of the Son of the Most High God. A sign is given to prove that nothing is impossible for God. Mary's kinswoman Elizabeth, thought to be sterile, has conceived a son in her old age. Mary is awestruck, but her only desire is to do what God requires. "I am the servant of the Lord. Let it be done to me as you say," she replies. One day Jesus will say that his mother's blessedness is not due to her maternity alone but because she hears the word of God and obeys it.

God is to be praised for having bestowed every spiritual blessing on all of us. Before the world began, God chose us to be holy and blameless. God's grace is more original than sin. It is God's will and pleasure for us to be adopted sons and daughters, brothers and sisters of Jesus. With our mother Mary we praise the divine favor conferred on us through Christ, God's beloved Son. We sing a new song! God has done wondrous things for Mary and for us. In the sight of all people, God has made salvation known, granted victory over sin through Mary's son.

To Consider

- Do I know that I am blessed in Christ?
- Have I responded to God's invitation to bear Christ to the world?
- How can I imitate Mary's servanthood?

To Pray

Pray Psalm 98: Mary, my mother, through your son, God's kindness and faithfulness have been revealed. All the ends of the earth see the salvation he brings.

Season of Christmas

Christmas — Mass of the Vigil (ABC)

Mt 1:1-25
  Isa 62:1-5; Ps 89; Acts 13:16-17,22-25

*"Look, the virgin shall conceive and bear a son,
    and they shall name him Emmanuel,"*
which means, "God is with us." — Mt 1:23

To Note

The first heresies did not so much deny Christ's divinity
as his true humanity (Gnostic Docetism, Arian). From the
apostolic age, the church has believed in the incarnation
of Christ, God's Son, who came in the "flesh." The first
council of Nicaea (325) formulated the creed that declares
the Son of God to be "begotten not made, of the same
substance (Greek: *homoousios*) as the Father," which expresses the unity of the Son and the Father. The *Catechism
of the Catholic Church* restates this ancient belief that Jesus
Christ "became truly man while remaining truly God.
Jesus Christ is true God and true man" (464).

To Understand

It is of Mary that Jesus the Messiah is born. Mary is God's
delight, espoused by the Spirit of God. When Joseph, her
betrothed, feels frightened and unworthy of so great a
privilege, God tells him to be brave and have confidence
in God's plans. The child brought forth is Emmanuel,
"God is with us." God is faithful. When we walk in darkness and desolation, God calls us by a new name: "My
Delight." When we feel worthless and forsaken, God calls
us "My Espoused." We are not abandoned but held ten-
derly in the hand of God like a royal crown with precious
jewels. Just as a bride brings happiness to her bridegroom,

so God delights in us. God wants to build us up when we have been brought low and to renew us in love. With the gift of such wondrous love, we cannot be silent. We sing, we rejoice, we shout in praise of God who is "Father," a "rock" of safety and refuge, the God who saves us.

Paul calls for a moment of silence while he recounts the story of God's tender mercy and kindness through all generations. When we were captive slaves in a far country, God saved us with an outstretched arm. God raised up David as our leader, a man after God's own heart. God promised David that his kingdom would endure forever. From this man's descendants, God brought forth Jesus, our savior, whose reign is without end. God was faithful to the covenant made with Abraham, Isaac, Jacob, Judah, and David. God was faithful to Mary and Joseph, to Paul, and to us, God's chosen ones. In Jesus, God is Emmanuel, with us, in us, and through us this holy day and all the seasons of our lives.

To Consider

- Do I feel loved by God?
- Have I thanked God for sending Jesus to us?
- For what am I most grateful today?
- How can I share this gift with others?

To Pray

Pray Psalm 89: Father God, thank you for sending your son Jesus to be our savior. I will sing your praises to all generations and rejoice in your goodness forever.

Christmas — Mass at Midnight (ABC)

Lk 2:1-14
  Isa 9:1-6; Ps 96; Titus 2:11-14

To you is born this day in the city of David a Savior, who is the Messiah, the Lord. — Lk 2:11

To Note

The tradition of displaying the Christmas scene with a manger began in Italy in December 1223. At the hermitage in Grecchio, Francis of Assisi celebrated midnight Mass by reenacting the first Christmas at Bethlehem. With fellow friars and neighbors, he assembled a cast of live animals and people in a cave. In this way, St. Francis encouraged the faithful to reflect on the love and poverty of the Holy Family. This Christmas custom of the crèche (French: "crib") continues in homes and parishes throughout the world.

To Understand

Like the shepherds who kept their watch, we wait in the dark of night. Gradually, a ray of light can be seen through the profound darkness—first a tiny flicker, then more light as a flame of hope is passed from one person to another. The grace of God has risen like the sun, offering salvation to all people. The one we awaited with longing has appeared. A new song can be heard throughout the land. What was whispered in the darkness becomes a joyful anthem: "A child is born to us, a son is given us!" The assembly blesses the divine names: "Wonderful! Counselor! Mighty God! Everlasting Father! Prince of Peace!"

Jesus comes into a world that is anything but peaceful. The land is occupied by a foreign tyrant. "Hail Caesar!" is the decree. Poor and laboring under a crushing tax, Joseph and Mary, who is heavy with child, make the long journey to Bethlehem, David's birthplace. Hospitality is the rule, but there is no room left in the places where travelers lodge. "Sorry, perhaps the next place will give you shelter." There is no welcome for the child of God as he enters a dark and weary world. "Do not be afraid!" God sends a message of hope to the poor and lowly. "This day a savior has been born." With the angelic host we praise God for bringing peace on earth to all of good will.

God's promise to David is fulfilled in the incarnation of Jesus Christ. The throne and scepter are passed to Jesus. He rules over God's kingdom with authority and wisdom. He teaches us how to reject ungodly ways. In Jesus' saving death we are made a people worthy to be called God's own. Jesus offers divine love to all, regardless of status or position. Our faithful Advocate contends against any power that keeps us in bondage. The yoke is lifted; the burden rests upon his shoulders. War and oppression are banished. The sign of his presence is peace. Let the heavens be glad and the earth rejoice. Today our Savior is born.

To Consider

- Have I made room in my heart for the coming of Christ, or is it too full of other things to welcome him?
- How can I bring others peace this day?

To Pray

Pray Psalm 96: Jesus, you are my Lord and Savior. You come to rule the world with justice. Day after day I will announce your wondrous deeds to all people.

Christmas — Mass at Dawn (ABC)

Lk 2:15-20
  Isa 62:11-12; Ps 97; Titus 3:4-7

*So they went with haste and found Mary and Joseph, and
the child lying in the manger. — Lk 2:16*

To Note

In the time of Jesus, shepherds were ranked with thieves
and tax collectors. Since they were not usually religiously
observant, they were deemed unfit to be part of the "righteous people." The inclusion of shepherds in the story of
Jesus' birth is a sign of his ministry to the poor and the
outcast. Jesus willingly associates with the *Anawim*, the
lowly and oppressed who had no one to rely on but God.
The shepherds are the first to hear of Jesus' birth. It is to
the poor that the reign of God is promised (Lk 6:20). They
are the first to respond to Jesus' glad tidings of redemption.

To Understand

Light dawns on the earth. Through the birth of Jesus,
God's loving kindness is fully revealed. We can't earn this
favor, nor do we deserve it. It is simply due to God's mercy.
Though undeserving, we are heirs of eternal life. In baptism we receive the gift of new birth in Jesus; in the Holy
Spirit we are renewed by God's love. While in the past we
may have felt like a deserted and forsaken city, we are
rebuilt into a worthy dwelling place of God.

There were many on that cold night in Bethlehem who
felt unworthy of God's attention. Among the poor and
despised are the shepherds living in the fields, outside the
city. Though their trade is essential, no upright person will

84

associate with them unless it is necessary. Yet the glorious light of heaven shines on these outcasts. It is to these lowly ones that God's messengers announce the incredible news that a savior has been born. When the light dims and the heavenly choir grows silent, the shepherds look at each another in amazement. "Can this really be true? Why would God bother to tell us and not the rich and important people?" Another suggests, "Let's not stand here wasting time! Let's go see for ourselves!"

It is true! We are among those privileged to see the savior whom God foretold. We are astonished. Where is the palace for such an important person? Why is a cave the birthplace of a king? How can a manger, a feeding trough for animals, be his throne? There is Mary, his mother, and Joseph, her spouse. They too are humble and poor. In the city, no one received them into their homes. Mary's eyes meet ours and we begin to understand. Her son comes for those who need a savior, who are hungry and waiting to be fed. He comes for those who have eyes and ears to perceive his coming. He comes to those who welcome and treasure God's gift in the cave of their hearts. With the poor we cry out with gladness: See, our Savior comes!

To Consider

- Has Jesus entered your home and heart this Christmas day?
- Have you welcomed his arrival?
- Have you opened your doors in hospitality to others?

To Pray

Pray Psalm 97: Lord, your light shines on us this day. We are glad and rejoice in your birth. We pray that all nations will see your glory.

Christmas — Mass during the Day (ABC)

Jn 1:1-18
  Isa 52:7-10; Ps 98; Heb 1:1-6

And the Word became flesh and lived among us, and we have seen his glory, the glory as of a father's only son, full of grace and truth. — Jn 1:14

To Note

Logos is a Greek term for "utterance" or "pronouncement." It corresponds to the Hebrew *memra*, "word," by which God acts in creation. The Vatican II Dogmatic Constitution on Divine Revelation, *Dei Verbum*, "exhorts all the Christian faithful...to learn the `surpassing knowledge of Jesus Christ' (Phil 3:8) by frequent reading of the divine Scriptures. `Ignorance of the Scriptures is ignorance of Christ' (St. Jerome)." The synod further reminds us "that prayer should accompany the reading of sacred Scripture...for `we speak to him when we pray; we listen to him when we read the divine oracles'" (25, St. Ambrose).

To Understand

We have watched through the night, and now with the dawn, a great light shines upon the earth. With our eyes we can see what our hearts longed for—the restoration of God's people. We raise a glad cry, "Here is your God who comes to save." In the sight of all people, God's might is shown. All the ends of the earth can see the power of God revealed through the savior's coming. He is the first-born of all who share his inheritance of eternal life. Through Jesus' birth and his saving death, we are cleansed of all unrighteousness. How beautiful is this message of peace and joy!

The inconceivable news is that God speaks with a human voice—like that of the watchman on Zion who proclaims deliverance for all who are held bound. We hear God's voice in the prophets, who promise salvation, and in John the Baptist, who testifies to the light that shatters our darkness. Even more amazingly, God speaks through a powerless infant who has no words. In Jesus, God cries full-throated. Jesus is the "word made flesh," who comes to dwell among us and in us. Jesus is more than an image or mirror of God; he is the *logos* of God, the ordering principle of the universe that sustains all things. Despite his transcendence, we can see, touch, and hear this "word" of God. In times past, we were too deaf to hear God's message. We were blind to God's presence. When our eyes and ears are opened, we can see Jesus and hear God speak. Jesus' words reveal the compassion and merciful love of God. His words are full of light, which is so powerful that no one can suppress it. His words are life-giving, setting us free from all that imprisons us. We who were once voiceless break out in song. With trumpet, harp, and horn we joyfully sing a new song of the saving power of God.

To Consider

- Have I heard the good news of salvation proclaimed today?
- Do I announce good or bad news to my family and friends?
- What is one good "word" that I can speak today?

To Pray

Pray Psalm 98: Lord, you have made your salvation known to all the ends of the earth. You remember your kindness and faithfulness toward us, your people.

Second Day in Octave of Christmas
(December 26)

Note: Today we remember St. Stephen, First Martyr.

Mt 10:17-22
  Acts 6:8-10, 7:54-59; Ps 31

You will be hated by all because of my name. But the one who endures to the end will be saved. — Mt 10:22

To Note

"Martyr" is a Greek word that means "witness," as in court. In the early church, many chose to suffer or die rather than give up their Christian principles, so the word took on its present meaning. The martyrdom of Stephen (Acts 7:54-60) and James the Apostle (Acts 12:1-2) conforms to the death of Jesus, who died for the benefit of others. During the third century, Romans engaged in organized persecution of the church. With the legalization of Christianity by Constantine (312), martyrdom declined but continues to occur whenever Christians confront oppression. Examples of modern martyrs are Dietrich Bonhoeffer in Nazi Germany; Martin Luther King, Jr., in the United States; and Archbishop Oscar Romero, priests, churchwomen, and lay people in El Salvador.

To Understand

It is the day after Christmas, the joyful celebration of the birth of Jesus, the prince of peace, when we are asked to look at the cost of discipleship. "Give me a little peace!" we groan. We'd rather sing another carol, have another egg nog, enjoy family and friends. Jesus wakes us up. The Christmas story isn't simply about a babe in a manger on a silent, holy night in a little town of Bethlehem. Christmas

88

is about Jesus becoming human to liberate humanity from injustice. The mystery of the crib is intimately connected with the mystery of the cross.

As Jesus sends his followers forth to preach the Gospel, he warns them of the opposition they will face. Their own people will charge them for being disloyal. They will be despised as heretics who violate the law of Moses. They will be hailed before the court and tortured by state and religious authorities. Hardest of all, they will be rejected by friends and family on account of Jesus.

Stephen is a member of the Jerusalem community, a Hellenist (a person of Greek language and culture) chosen by the apostles to help minister to the needs of the Greek-speaking Christians. Although appointed to the mundane job of distributing food and goods, Stephen shows himself to be an eloquent spokesman for the church. Because he radically opposes those who use their office to exploit people, he is stoned to death. As he dies, Stephen commends his spirit to God and prays, as Jesus did, for the forgiveness of his persecutors. Through Jesus' presence in our lives, we are called to help transform the world, no matter how great the demands or difficult the task.

To Consider

- How is Christ incarnated in my life?
- Am I living the paschal mystery by standing up for what I believe?

To Pray

Pray Psalm 31: Jesus, you are my refuge and my stronghold, my rock and my fortress. I place my life in your hands, trusting that you will lead and guide me to safety.

Third Day in Octave of Christmas (December 27)

Note: Today we remember St. John, Apostle and Evangelist.

Jn 20:2-8
   1 Jn 1:1-4; Ps 97

Then the other disciple, who reached the tomb first, also went in, and he saw and believed. — Jn 20:8

To Note

"Evangelist" is derived from the Greek word *euaggelion*, "to announce the good news." It is a title for early Christian preachers such as the apostles, their disciples, and the authors of the Gospels. In the first millennium, the church carried Christ's mandate "to the ends of the earth." In the second millenium, Vatican Council II declared that the very "nature" of the church is to evangelize (*Ad Gentes* 2). After the council, the bishops met to consider the task of evangelization. Pope Paul VI expressed these reflections in his apostolic exhortation *On Evangelization in the Modern World*. As we approach a new millennium, Pope John Paul II calls lay people to be involved in a renewed commitment to the mission of the church in *Evangelization 2000!*

To Understand

For John, the incarnation is not just a theological notion. John personally experienced Jesus in his human existence. John looked upon Jesus with his own eyes. With his own ears, he heard Jesus speak. "Our hands have touched," he poignantly declares. This "word made flesh" is the "word of life" to which John testifies. This was John's purpose in writing; it was his mission on earth.

John is the last evangelist to write a Gospel. He writes toward the end of the first century to a maturing community interested in the meaning of the events in Christ's life. Like the other evangelists, John writes from the perspective of the resurrection. John helps us to see the significance of the empty tomb that he and Peter witnessed.

It is the first day of the week, the beginning of a new creation, a world renewed through Christ's death and resurrection. Mary Magdalene, the first witness of the resurrection, runs to tell the other disciples that the stone has been removed from the tomb. Peter and John hurry to see for themselves. (Who would believe the testimony of a woman?) Though they run side by side, when they arrive at the tomb, John defers to Peter, the leader of the apostles, the head of the church. Peter carefully notes the burial clothes lying on the ground, but he is slow to understand the meaning. John sees the same things, yet he believes. John understands that the empty tomb points to the new life that he and all others will experience. Like Mary Magdalene, we may wonder where the Lord is in our life. Like Peter, we may ponder the facts. Like John, we can see and believe!

To Consider

- Have I experienced the risen Lord today, or do I only see an empty tomb?
- How can I share the good news of Christ in my life?

To Pray

Pray Psalm 97: Lord, may all people rejoice in your coming. May your justice rule over the earth, bringing joy and banishing darkness.

Fourth Day in Octave of Christmas (December 28)

Note: Today we remember the Holy Innocents, Martyrs.

Mt 2:13-18
  1 Jn 1:5-2:2; Ps 124

A voice was heard in Ramah,
  wailing and loud lamentation,
Rachel weeping for her children;
  she refused to be consoled, because they are no more.
— Mt 2:18

To Note

Abortion by its very nature is the destruction of innocent human life. Life begins at the moment of conception; there is no mutation in the identity of the unborn from one month to the next. No matter how conception occurs, a child is created in the image of God and bears the seed of immortality. The so-called "Freedom of Choice Act" would allow abortion, through all nine months of a pregnancy, to be an absolute right without any moral consequence. The alternative is to provide legislation and social services to assist mother and child. Freedom of choice is not doing what is most convenient but doing what is right.

To Understand

John refuses to buy into the prophets of doom and gloom. "God is light," he says. "There is no darkness in God." We must not walk in the dark when there is the opportunity to walk in light. We do not have to be afraid of the darkness from within or from without. We have companions on the journey who will help us bear witness to the Gospel we profess.

There are always wise men and women who follow the heavenly light, like the Magi who searched for one who would rule the world with peace and justice. They bring gifts of great wealth and beauty befitting a king. Yet with the gift is also the portent of death. No sooner did the Magi leave when Joseph hears the ominous message: "Get up and flee with the child and his mother. There is one searching for the child who wants to destroy him!" Terrified, Joseph does as he is told. When Herod realizes that he has been deceived, he wants blood revenge. One child is not enough. Are two, three, one hundred, one thousand, one million enough? Countless innocent victims of violence, war, poverty, crime, and abortion have been sacrificed on the altar of selfishness, greed, hatred, and power, destroying the good gifts God gives us. With Mary and Joseph and the Magi, we must "return by another way," follow a path of peace, not violence. Jesus accompanies us every step of the way. He is our intercessor who offers himself for our failings. If we confess our faults and reform our lives, we can be confident that his love and mercy will be with us.

To Consider

- What can I do to advocate respect for life?
- How can I overcome darkness in my community?
- How can I bring Christ's light to the world?

To Pray

Pray Psalm 124: Savior God, if you were not with us, we would be swept away in the torrent against us. Our help is in the name of the Lord, who made heaven and earth.

Fifth Day in Octave of Christmas
(December 29)

Lk 2:22-35
  1 Jn 2:3-11; Ps 96

Then Simeon blessed them and said to his mother Mary,
"This child is destined for the falling and the rising of many
in Israel, and to be a sign that will be opposed." — Lk 2:34

To Note

A canticle is a sacred chant or hymn of praise or love
directed toward God. Canticles have been incorporated
into the Divine Office (The Liturgy of the Hours) of the
Church. There are fourteen canticles from the Hebrew
Scriptures and three "Gospel" or "evangelical" canticles:
the Magnificat (Lk 1:46-55), Benedictus (Lk 1:68-79), and
the Nunc Dimittis (Lk 2:29-32). The title "Nunc Dimittis" is taken from the first two words in the Latin version
of the hymn "Now dismiss." The Canticle of Simeon is
said at Night Prayer, expressing faith in God's work of
salvation and asking protection as we sleep and wake.

To Understand

On a bright and sunny day, we may say, "The sun is
blinding me." John says that darkness can blind us, too.
When we walk in spiritual darkness, we do not know where
we are going. We are confused and unsure whether we are
following Christ. John says when we walk in the light of
Christ, we have a good idea of where we are going. That's
a real challenge but, as always, Jesus sums it up in love.
We can't claim to follow him if we have malice toward our
brothers and sisters. John says the law of love is nothing

94

new; love was always the purpose of God's commands. At the same time, love is always new. Every day offers a new opportunity to love as Jesus loves.

Mary and Joseph are faithful to the commands of God. According to the law, the couple presents the infant Jesus in the temple and fulfills the sacred purification rites. According to the law, a woman was considered ritually impure for forty days after the birth of a son. After this time, she was required to offer a year-old lamb as an offering and a turtledove or pigeon as an expiation for sin. Mary and Joseph are poor; they can only afford two turtledoves or pigeons. But Mary holds the sacrificial Lamb of God in her arms, the perfect offering to God. In the temple that day is a man named Simeon, who faithfully awaits the redemption of Israel. Though Simeon is old, his eyesight is good enough to see the promised Messiah, who will restore the hope of his people. Simeon thanks God for allowing him to live to see the "revealing light" to all people. Simeon blesses the parents but addresses his words to Mary. As the mother of the one through whom salvation enters the world, she will share the suffering of her son.

To Consider

- Do I recognize the fulfillment of God's promises in my life? Have I given thanks for this gift?
- How is the faithful love of the Holy family an example to me?

To Pray

Pray Psalm 96: Lord, day after day I sing a new song of your love. Today I will announce your salvation among your people and tell of your glorious deeds.

Sixth Day in Octave of Christmas (December 30)

Note: If Christmas fell on a Sunday, the feast of the Holy Family is celebrated December 30.

Lk 2:36-40
  1 Jn 2:12-17; Ps 96

The child grew and became strong, filled with wisdom; and the favor of God was upon him. — Lk 2:40

To Note

The "Dogmatic Constitution on the Church" (*Lumen Gentium*) declares that Jesus Christ, himself a model of perfection, "preached holiness of life" (Mt 5:48). The document clearly states that "all Christians in any state or walk of life are called to the fullness of Christian life and to the perfection of love." By living a holy life, a Christian fosters a "more human manner of life" in society. The church summons the "People of God" to follow in Christ's footsteps and to conform their will to God in everything, "wholeheartedly devoting themselves to the glory of God and to the service of their neighbor" (40).

To Understand

Simeon isn't the only one who blesses Jesus on the day of his presentation in the temple. Another elderly person, a widow by the name of Anna, is also there. Like Simeon, Anna was a holy person who dedicated her life to prayer and service. She spent her time fasting and praying, waiting for the salvation of Israel. Anna was a "prophetess," a spokesperson for God like the prophets of old. Anna happens to pass by as Simeon is blessing Mary, Joseph, and the child Jesus. Because she spent so many years in prayer, Anna recognizes this moment of revelation. She gives thanks to God and tells everyone she meets about the deliverance that will come through this anointed child. When the Holy Family fulfills all the requirements of the law, they return to their home in Nazareth. There Jesus grows physically, intellectually, and spiritually. As a young man, Jesus will return to the temple for the Passover feast. As an adult, he will claim the temple as his own, establishing it as a house of prayer for all God's people. For now, it is Jesus' task to remain with his family, be obedient to them, and grow strong in God's favor and grace.

John writes to all God's people—parents, young adults, children—all who strive to follow Christ as a disciple. A disciple is one of the "little ones" whom Christ praises as being open to God's revelation when the wise and learned are not. Whatever our age or status in life, each of us can be of service to the Lord. Because these disciples are faithful to the Word of God, they can conquer evil. They have no attachment to the world and its values. These are only an "empty show," which cannot allure or entice a true follower of Christ. The world with its seductions is passing away, but the one who does God's will endures forever.

To Consider

- Do I recognize the answer to my prayers when I see it?
- In what ways can I be of service to families or to the elderly and widowed of my parish?

To Pray

Pray Psalm 96: Lord, we give you the glory and praise due your name. May heaven and earth rejoice for you rule your people with justice.

Seventh Day in Octave of Christmas
(December 31)

Jn 1:1-18
  1 Jn 2:18-21; Ps 96

The light shines in the darkness, and the darkness did not overcome it. — Jn 1:5

To Note

The word "antichrist," mentioned only in the letters of John (1 Jn 2:18,22; 4:3; 2 Jn 7), refers to one who denies that Jesus Christ came in the flesh as God's Son. The word does not appear in the Book of Revelation, although the "antichrist" has been identified with the "Beast," the deceiver and blasphemer who leads people astray in the last days (Rev 13:11-14). The word also suggests Paul's "man of lawlessness," who proclaims himself to be God (1 Thess 2:3-10). Throughout history the antichrist was associated with historical figures such as the Roman Emperor Nero, who persecuted Christians, or the heretic Arius, who taught that the Son is inferior to the Father. At times, anti-Catholic groups have declared that the pope is the antichrist. Catholic tradition sees the antichrist as any persons or forces that work against the will of God.

To Understand

The prologue to John's Gospel is a mystical hymn to the eternal Christ, who comes with life and light to conquer death and darkness. John does not record the nativity of the Lord. John returns to the beginning of time. The pre-existent Christ becomes human and dwells on earth. Just as God dwelt with Israel in the wilderness tabernacle,

Christ "pitches his tent" or "tabernacles" himself among us. At the moment of creation, God overpowers darkness by speaking a word that brings forth light. In a sin-weary world, God's light shines its brightest through Jesus Christ.

John the Baptist is a "lamp" lighting the way for the transcendent light emanating from Jesus. Though John announces a "message" of repentance, Jesus is God's "Word," who comes to enlighten his people. All who believe in Jesus find life in him. Through baptism they are empowered to become "children of God." Though Jesus is the gift-bearer of God's eternal love, many refuse to believe in him. Some separate themselves from Christ and his church and proclaim a false Gospel. Such "antichrists" espouse darkness over the Word, which brings light. Just as falsehood has nothing in common with the truth, an "antichrist" has nothing in common with the faithful of Christ, who have true knowledge of God. Perhaps those who walk away from the light never really belonged to the faith community. If they did belong, why did they leave? If we ask this of others, we need to examine ourselves. Do we bring light or darkness to our communities?

To Consider

- Do I feel separated from or connected to the Christian community?
- Am I a "light-bearer" or do I spread false teachings?
- Have I announced God's salvation to those who feel alienated?

To Pray

Pray Psalm 96: Lord, all creation sings your praise; all lands bless your name. You come to rule the world with justice and faithfulness.

Sunday in Octave of Christmas, Holy Family (A)

Note: If Christmas fell on a Sunday, the Feast of the Holy Family is celebrated December 30.

Mt 2:13-15,19-23
    Sir 3:2-6,12-14; Ps 128; Col 3:12-21

Then Joseph got up, took the child and his mother, and went to the land of Israel. — Mt 2:21

To Note

Pope John Paul II's pro-life encyclical states that "the gospel of life is at the heart of Jesus' message," which should be "preached as good news to the people of every age and culture." The Holy Father says that on the "eve of the Third Millennium, the challenge facing us is an arduous one." Because of threats to human life, the pope urges a "general mobilization of consciences and a united ethical effort to activate a great campaign in support of life. All together, we must build a new culture of life...capable of bringing about a serious and courageous cultural dialogue among all parties" ("The Gospel of Life," *Evangelium Vitae*, 1995)

To Understand

Dreams can be fearful nightmares, but they can also contain messages of hope. Joseph, the beloved son of Jacob, is a dreamer who receives divine messages about his forthcoming role among the tribes. Because of his brothers' jealousy, Joseph is sold into slavery in Egypt. Once there, he rises to power and, years later, is able to save his family from starvation. When a new pharaoh comes to power,

Joseph is no longer remembered, and Egypt becomes a place of enslavement for God's people. It is in this land that Moses is raised. But Moses has to flee the pharaoh's wrath when he kills an Egyptian whom he sees abusing a fellow Hebrew. Moses returns to Egypt when those who sought his life are dead. In obedience to God, Moses leads his people from slavery to the promised land.

Though Egypt was a place of bondage for God's people, it was a place of refuge for the holy family in a time of great danger. King Herod sees the birth of Jesus, "the newborn king," as a threat to his throne, and he determines to kill him. The Lord appears to Joseph in a dream; he is told to take Mary and the child and flee to Egypt. In Herod's malicious attempt to do away with Jesus, he murders innocent children. When Herod dies, the Lord tells Joseph to return to "the land of Israel" because those who sought the child's life are dead. In the Holy Family's flight and return, Jesus relives Israel's deliverance from Egypt in the Exodus. Obedient to God's will, Jesus is the new Moses who liberates his people from all that enslaves them. When we obey God, we find that, though the path is often difficult and unexpected, a future full of hope is assured.

To Consider

- How is Joseph's obedience to God an example for my life?
- Do I listen for God's direction in my life?
- What is the outcome when I refuse to follow God's will?

To Pray

Pray Psalm 128: Holy Family, I am happiest when I live according to God's will. My family is blessed, and our lives are fruitful when we walk in God's ways.

Sunday in Octave of Christmas, Holy Family (B)

Note: If Christmas fell on a Sunday, the Feast of the Holy Family is celebrated December 30.

Lk 2:22-40
   Sir 3:2-6,12-14; Ps 128; Col 3:12-21

And the child's father and mother were amazed at what was being said about him. — Lk 2:33

To Note

The U.S. Bishops' Pastoral Message to Families states that "being open to new life signals trust in the God who ultimately creates and sustains all life." Bearing a child is "the beginning of a lifetime commitment: nurturing, teaching, disciplining and, finally, letting go of a child—as he or she follows a new and perhaps uncharted way of love." Each generation is challenged to pass on its "wisdom and the faith of the Church, providing countercultural messages about poverty, consumerism, sexuality and racial justice" ("Follow the Way of Love," 1994).

To Understand

Simeon and Anna are old. They spend their days fasting and praying in the temple, awaiting the redemption of Israel. When they see a young man and woman and their child performing the customary purification rites, they have a message for the couple. What can these old folks say to the younger generation? Will it be relevant? Will the young listen? The sage Sirach advises the young to be considerate of the old. Mary and Joseph are open to God's message, no matter how challenging or demanding. The words Simeon speaks are not something a young family

102

wants to hear. Many will oppose their child, and Mary's heart will be pierced with a sword of sorrow. Yet the message contains a hopeful promise. Their son is destined to be "the glory" of Israel, a "revealing light" to all people.

It is of no importance how young or old we are, how rich or poor, or what status we hold—we are all God's chosen ones. When we are baptized in Christ, we remove the "garments" of our former way of life and are "clothed" in love, mercy, kindness, humility, meekness, and patience. This is no easy garment to wear. It means we must be like Jesus, forgiving grievances and putting up with one another. Whatever we do, in speech or action, we should do all in the name of Jesus, our Lord.

Mary, Joseph, and Jesus show us that words are not enough. Like them, we must be faithful, holy members of God's family, worshiping and celebrating together, loving and honoring one another. The holy family gives us courage to be obedient to God's Word, no matter what it entails. Like them, we must dedicate our lives to truth and justice despite the hostility and conflict in the world. As a holy family, we must allow peace to reign in our hearts.

To Consider

- How does my parish family reach out to the elderly and infirm?
- What can these people teach me?
- What gift can I share with them?

To Pray

Pray Psalm 128: Holy Family, as we enjoy the fruits of our labors, help us to share our blessings with all who live in loneliness, hunger, poverty, and fear.

Sunday in Octave of Christmas, Holy Family (C)

Note: If Christmas fell on a Sunday, the Feast of the Holy Family is celebrated on December 30.

Lk 2:41-52
   Sir 3:2-6,12-14; Ps 128; Col 3:12-21

Then he went down with them and came to Nazareth, and was obedient to them. His mother treasured all these things in her heart. — Lk 2:51

To Note

The U.S. Bishops' Pastoral Message to Families says that "what you do in your family to create a community of love, to help each other to grow and to serve those in need is critical, not only for your own sanctification but also for the strength of society and our Church. It is a participation in the work of the Lord, a sharing in the mission of the Church. It is holy" ("Follow the Way of Love," 1994).

To Understand

We do not always grasp the significance of events in our lives; like Mary, we must ponder their meaning. Each year, Mary and Joseph go to Jerusalem to celebrate the Passover, the feast that commemorates their deliverance from slavery. The journey is usually uneventful. This year, Jesus has come of age, and he travels with them. On their return journey, Mary and Joseph assume that he is with relatives and friends in the caravan. After a day's travel, they are alarmed to discover that Jesus is not among them. Their search is frantic and desperate. Finally, they retrace their steps, returning to the Holy City.

It is the third day before they find him. Jesus is in the temple, where he had been all along, listening and asking questions of the scholars and teachers. Everyone is amazed by his wisdom—everyone but his parents. They are distraught and upset. "Why did you do this, son?" Mary asks in dismay. "Can't you see that your father and I have been looking everywhere for you in sorrow?" Jesus' answer pierces her heart like Simeon's promised sword. "Did you not know that I *had* to be in *my Father's* house?"

There will be other Passover pilgrimages, and there will be one final journey. This last time, Jesus will travel with a family of disciples. The feast of liberation will be a pass-over to suffering and death. For three days, the disciples will agonize over the fact that Jesus is not with them. His mother will participate in the suffering of her sons and daughters. It is the risen Christ who will find *them*, and he will explain that he *had* to return to his *Father*, where he continues to intercede for God's people.

To Consider

- Am I able to discover the purpose of events in my life when I reflect on their meaning?
- Do I continue to search for the Lord in times of distress and trouble?

To Pray

Pray Psalm 128: Holy Family, teach us daily to walk the journey through life as faithful sons and daughters, so we might receive the blessings God has promised.

Octave of Christmas,
Solemnity of Mary, Mother of God (ABC)

Lk 2:16-21
 Num 6:22-27; Ps 67; Gal 4:4-7

But Mary treasured all these words and pondered them in her heart. — Lk 2:19

To Note

One of the Marian titles is "Theotokos," a Greek word that means "God-bearer," expressing the fact that Mary gave birth to Jesus, the Son of God. The Latin equivalent is "Deigenetrix," "Mother of God." Nestorius, Patriarch of Constantinople (428-31), expressed reservations about the title, fearing that it threatened the full and distinct divinity and humanity of Christ. The third ecumenical council of Ephesus (431) was convoked to settle the debate. By declaring Mary to be Mother of God, the council acknowledged Jesus Christ to be "one and the same" divine person. This Christological teaching paved the way for the council of Chalcedon (451), which affirmed the one person of Christ in his two natures, divine and human.

To Understand

God's favor and light shine upon a dark yet hope-filled world. The time has come for the old to give way to the new. Everything is turned upside down in this blessed age. The law bows to grace. The knee bends not before a king on a throne but before a simple family. The maidservant of the Lord is the Mother of God. Salvation comes not with ceremony, pomp, and wealth but in a stable filled with animals, dirt, and excrement.

Shepherds are unaware of these conditions; this is the ordinary state of their lives. They do not see just a baby lying in a manger. The angelic messengers prepared them for what they would see: their savior, their Messiah and Lord. With their own ears they heard the message. With eyes of faith they behold the one who gives life to the world. With awe and joy they glorify and praise God for all they have heard and seen. All who hear their report are astonished.

Mary ponders these things, too. She has seen and heard more than the rest. In her grace-filled heart, she reflects on God's gracious gift. Mary's child is to be named "Jesus," the one who saves and liberates his people. For now, she must submit her son to the law. Though son of God, circumcision makes him an official member of God's human family. The covenant is sealed with pain and blood. As Mary cradles her wailing infant, she knows that one day his cry will proclaim peace and justice to the world. The mother of the one who brings salvation has begun to share his suffering and passion.

To Consider

- Do I ponder the events in my life to discover their meaning?
- How does Mary "mother" me in my own times of pain and sorrow?
- Do I embrace others in their suffering?

To Pray

Pray Psalm 67: Mary, Mother of God and my mother, pray that God will bless us with mercy. May your humble way be known upon the earth.

Christmas Weekday before Epiphany
(January 2)

Jn 1:19-28
  1 Jn 2:22-28; Ps 98

*John answered them, "I baptize with water. Among you
stands one whom you do not know." — Jn 1:26*

To Note

"Christ" is not Jesus' last name. Mary and Joseph were not
Mr. and Mrs. Christ. "The Christ" is a title meaning "the
anointed one" (Greek: *Christos*; Hebrew: *Mâshiah*, "Messiah"). The use of "Christ" as a proper name became
common after the death of Jesus. We see this particularly
in the writings of Paul, either before the name of Jesus—Christ Jesus (Phil 1:8)— or after—Jesus Christ (Phil
1:11). In the Hebrew Scriptures we see the title "the
Lord's anointed," used for kings whose investiture was
marked by the anointing with oil (1 Kings 1:39). At times,
prophets and priests were also anointed (1 Kings 19:16;
Lev 4:3). Biblical messianism, the tradition that God's
anointed one delivers his people from suffering and injustice, finds unique fulfillment in Jesus.

To Understand

John, the elder of his community, writes a letter to counter-
attack those who spread falsehood and create disunity in
the church. "Who is the liar?" he asks those who disregard
the true nature of Jesus Christ. Anyone who denies that
Jesus is "the Christ" is the "antichrist." Anyone who
refuses to believe that Jesus came in the flesh is a false
prophet who has separated from the believing community.

Those who do not confess the incarnate Son do not have the Father either. John appeals to the faithful remnant who "have the anointing" of the Spirit to abide in the truth that comes from the Spirit. Through baptism, God made a promise of eternal life. They do not need a new teaching. They can have confidence in the authentic tradition they have received from the beginning.

John the Baptist appears in the desert as the righteous herald of truth who prepares the way for the coming of the anointed one of God. John does not lie to those who ask his identity and mission. "Are you the Messiah?" they demand. "No," John decisively answers. "Who then, Elijah?" another asks. "No." "Are you the prophet?" they persist. "No," John says again. Now that he has told them who he is not, he tells them who he is. John has been sent by God to give testimony to the light that comes into the world through Jesus. John is a voice loudly announcing the coming of the Messiah of God. "If you are not the Messiah," some argue, "why do you baptize?" John says that he baptizes with water as a sign of repentance, but they are blind to the one coming after him. John may be a humble servant, but he is also a powerful voice that challenges us to believe.

To Consider

- Do others recognize the presence of Jesus in my life?
- In what ways do I proclaim his presence?
- Have I been a source of unity or disunity in my parish?

To Pray

Pray Psalm 98: St. John the Baptist, help me to announce the saving power of God. May all the ends of the earth see the salvation of our God.

Christmas Weekday before Epiphany
(January 3)

Jn 1:29-34
  1 Jn 2:29-3:6; Ps 98

He on whom you see the Spirit descend and remain is the one
who baptizes with the Holy Spirit. — Jn 1:33

To Note

The dove is the bird most often mentioned in the Bible.
The dove is a sign of God's love (Song 2:14; 5:2) and of the
new creation (Gen 8:8-12). The dove was the offering of
the poor in the purification rites of the temple (Lev 5:7;
12:8; Lk 2:24). The visible descent of the Holy Spirit
occurs in the form of a dove at Jesus' baptism, identifying
him as the promised bearer of the Holy Spirit. The dove
was a symbol of baptism for early Christians. The epiclesis
is a prayer recited before or after the words of institution
asking the Holy Spirit to descend upon and dwell within
the bread and wine and the congregation.

To Understand

John the elder is sadly aware of the divisions in his community. The conflict is a battle between the "children of
God" and those "begotten of the evil one." John says that
if anyone claims to know God yet is disobedient to God's
laws, then that person contradicts the truth by his or her
actions. John reminds God's faithful children of the tre-
mendous privilege and responsibility they have in baptism. Just as natural children resemble their parents, so too
children of God should favor their divine parent. They
must be righteous, virtuous, honest, and just because those

110

are God's attributes. The reason the world does not recognize the children of God is because they do not know God's Son, Jesus. Jesus is our elder brother who came into the world to enable us to see God and to take away our sins so we can be like God. Though we are mere children at the present, we are gradually conforming our lives to God's will. Like children, we must be obedient to God, who is our Father.

John the Baptist baptizes with the waters of repentance so that others might recognize Jesus. At first, John has trouble discerning Jesus as God's anointed one, but now his eyes are open. John recognized Jesus' true identity the moment the Spirit of God descended "like a dove" upon Jesus at his baptism. When John sees this, he knows that this is the moment of God's new creation, a sign of God's love. Jesus is God's chosen one. Jesus comes with the purifying grace of the Holy Spirit to reveal God's presence to all God's children. It is exciting to wonder if we will be like Jesus when we grow to maturity.

To Consider

- How has the grace of baptism given me power over sin in my life?
- Through my baptism, have I become a messenger of Jesus to my community?

To Pray

Pray Psalm 98: Jesus, I sing a new song because of your presence in my life. Help me to tell everyone of the victory you have won for me.

Christmas Weekday before Epiphany (January 4)

Jn 1:35-42
  1 Jn 3:7-10; Ps 98

"Come and see." — Jn 1:39

To Note

Oil was used for anointing the body in the arid Middle East. Because of its soothing qualities, oil was used for medicinal purposes (Lk 10:34). Oil was used on festive occasions and for burial (Mk 16:1). People refrained from its use in times of fasting (Mt 6:17) and mourning (2 Sam 14:2). The woman who anointed Jesus in anticipation of his burial did so as an extravagant gesture of love (Jn 12:7). Oil was used in religious rites for healing (Jas 5:14). Persons, objects, the tabernacle, and temple furnishings were anointed as a sign of their dedication to God. Holy oils are sacramentals blessed by a bishop. The three types are oil of catechumens, holy chrism, and oil of the sick.

To Understand

"Look!" John says again. "There is the lamb of God!" Like children playing follow the leader, we line up behind Jesus as he blazes a trail ahead. He turns and sees his flock coming after him as sheep follow the shepherd. "What are you looking for?" he asks. This is no longer a game; Jesus is dead serious. No one has asked us this before. We stop and think, but we can't come up with a reasonable answer. "Teacher," we stammer, "where do you stay?" We're tired of following false leaders. Deep within we long for safe pastures, a home where we can be secure forever. "Come and see!" Jesus invites us. Eagerly we go with him to stay a day, a week, a month, a year, a lifetime.

One of those following Jesus is Andrew, the brother of Simon. Andrew can't wait to tell Simon of his discovery. "We've found the Messiah, God's anointed one!" he declares, excitedly dragging Simon to meet Jesus. Jesus looks at the big fisherman and calls him by a new name. Simon becomes a new creation, with a new identity and a new vocation. He is named Cephas, Peter the rock, a strong foundation for Jesus' church.

John writes to the church as it faces new threats to its permanency and stability. "Little ones," John says to his flock, "let no one deceive you." He says that there is a simple test for recognizing true followers of Jesus. Those whose deeds are holy resemble God's son, who is holy. They are begotten of God; they are God's children. Jesus came into the world to destroy the works of the evil one, who wants to separate and divide God's children. Anyone who fails to love one's brother and sister does not belong to God's family. Jesus calls us as he called his first disciples. If we are willing to follow him, our identity is changed too. In our baptism we are named, washed, and anointed. Then, like Jesus, we can invite others to follow him, too.

To Consider

- Have I taken time each day to be with Jesus?
- How has this changed me?
- Do I invite others to "come and see" for themselves?

To Pray

Pray Psalm 98: Lord Jesus, in you I am a new creation, a child of God who sings songs of joy proclaiming God's saving power.

Christmas Weekday before Epiphany
(January 5)

Jn 1:43-51
  1 Jn 3:11-21; Ps 100

[Jesus] found Philip and said to him, "Follow me."
— *Jn 1:43*

To Note

In the Bible, names are full of meaning and often descriptive of an individual's personality. Changing one's name gives that person a new identity or status. Abram's name was changed to Abraham, Jacob's to Israel, Simon's to Peter, each indicating a call and vocation. At baptism, a Christian name is usually given to the one receiving the sacrament. One becomes "*christ*ened," having a new identity in Christ. The chosen name may be that of a saint, who becomes one's "patron." We strive in our spiritual lives to imitate the saints' virtues and moral values.

To Understand

"Follow me!" Jesus tells Philip of Bethsaida, a neighbor of Peter and Andrew. When Philip receives his call, he goes to find his friend Nathanael, who is dozing under a fig tree. "Nathanael!" Philip announces. "We've found the one Moses spoke of, the one the prophets foretold. It is Jesus of Nazareth, son of Joseph!" What nonsense, thinks Nathanael. How can the Messiah come from Nazareth? Surely the Messiah will come from Jerusalem, David's city. Nathanael casts a skeptical eye at Philip, "Can anything good come from Nazareth?" Philip knows no argument will persuade him. "Come see for yourself."

114

When Jesus sees Nathanael, he declares, "This man is a true Israelite, a man of no guile." Nathanael's ego swells. "Israel" was Jacob's name after God changed it. Israel was the father of many people, but he was also a trickster who deceived his brother Esau and uncle Laban. God's choices were always amazing. Nathanael wonders, "Could God be calling me too?" He asks, "How do you know me?" Jesus answers, "Before Philip called you, I saw you under the fig tree." Nathanael is aghast. "Rabbi... Teacher! You are the Son of God! You are the king of Israel!" Nathanael believes because of Jesus' personal knowledge of him, but he will see greater things. Like Jacob/Israel, who saw the heavenly ladder with God's messengers ascending and descending, Nathanael will witness Jesus' words and works as he joins heaven and earth by his coming.

John writes to his church, reminding them of Jesus' commands to love one another the way Jesus loved by laying down our lives for one another. In Christ, we are committed to each other in deed and truth. There must be no guile in us as we follow Jesus.

To Consider

- Have I taken the risk to invite those who are reluctant to follow Christ?
- At times, am I unwilling to follow him?
- Am I dedicated to serving my brothers and sisters in need?

To Pray

Pray Psalm 100: Lord, we are your people, the flock that you tend. Help us to serve one another with a joyful, grateful heart.

Christmas Weekday before Epiphany (January 6)

Mk 1:7-11
  1 Jn 5:5-13; Ps 147

I have baptized you with water; but he will baptize you with the Holy Spirit. — Mk 1:8

To Note

In the Bible, water has several important meanings: fertility and birth, danger and cleansing. At the moment of creation, the world emerges from the chaotic waters. A sinful world is punished by a flood (Gen 6-9). Moses' name means "drawn out" of the water, a birth metaphor (Ex 2:1-10). The Israelite nation is born by crossing the Red Sea (Ex 14:26-31). God gives water to a thirsty people in the arid desert (Ex 17:1-7; Jn 4:7-10). A river will one day flow from Jerusalem (Ezek 47:1-12; Rev 22:1-2). Jesus walks upon the water, signifying his divine sovereignty (Mt 14:22-33). Water is a key element in purification and healing rites (Num 8:5-7; 2 Kings 5:14; Jn 2:6; 5:2-7). Baptism, like the Jewish conversion rite of immersion, signifies spiritual rebirth (Jn 3:5; Rom 6:4; Gal 3:26-27).

To Understand

John writes to help his community understand the responsibility they have as a people baptized in Christ. Baptism isn't simply a ritual symbolizing new life. To be "born" in the baptismal bath means to die to one's former way of life to rise to a new life in Christ. This life requires a daily following of Jesus' way of the cross, sharing his passion as well as his resurrection. For many, entering the Christian life meant possible martyrdom to the faith. The spirit testifies to this truth. Jesus Christ brings us life through water and blood. John emphasizes this, "not in water only, but in water *and* in blood."

John the Baptist knows that the pathway he prepares for Jesus will lead to both their deaths. Yet John willingly proclaims the good news that in Jesus the kingdom of God has come. John considers himself unworthy of performing the lowly servant's task of untying his master's sandals to cleanse his feet from the long journey. The baptism John performs is a rite of purification, signifying a willingness to reform one's life so that sins might be forgiven. John heralds the one who will baptize with the transforming power of the Holy Spirit. Jesus humbly submits to John's baptism. When Jesus comes up from the waters of the Jordan River, the heavens are torn open, and the Spirit of God pours forth like a spring rain. The Spirit lights upon Jesus, and a heavenly voice is heard confirming Jesus' identity: "You are my beloved Son. On you my favor rests." In baptism, we step from the sinful waters into the cleansing stream of God's grace. Washed and renewed, we hear our name called. We are amazed that God's favor rests on us, too.

To Consider

- In what ways do I live my baptismal call?
- Have I experienced both dying and rising in Christ?
- How have I given testimony to my new life in Christ?

To Pray

Pray Psalm 147: Lord, you have blessed your children. You strengthen us and give us peace. Help us to heed your voice.

Christmas Weekday before Epiphany
(January 7)

Jn 2:1-12
  1 Jn 5:14-21; Ps 149

*Everyone serves the good wine first, and then the inferior
wine after the guests have become drunk. But you have kept
the good wine until now. — Jn 2:10*

To Note

In the Bible, wine is a sign of the messianic reign when the
Lord provides "rich food" and "choice wine" for all (Isa
25:6). For centuries, Christians received both the consecrated bread and wine in communion, but by the end of
the thirteenth century a change in practice developed.
Fear of disease and of spilling the wine and the doctrine
that Christ is "whole and entire" in either form contributed
to the demise of the cup. Today, "Holy Communion,
considered as a sign, has a fuller form when it is received
under both kinds....Moreover, it is more clearly shown how
the new and eternal covenant is ratified in the blood of the
Lord, as it also expresses the relation of the eucharistic
banquet to the eschatological banquet in the Kingdom of
the Father" (*Constitution on the Sacred Liturgy* 32).

To Understand

Water is changed to wine! People of disbelief are trans-
formed into people of faith! Which is the greater miracle?
The age of the Messiah has come, its signs manifested in
Jesus' wondrous deeds. The first "sign" is the miracle of
the wine at the wedding feast at Cana. Jesus' mother,
Mary, is present at this first "hour" of her son's glory, as

she will be at his final "hour," his glorification on the cross. It is a small wedding in an insignificant village. The guests have traveled many miles, and there must be enough food and drink at the banquet, which will last several days. But to the bridal party's embarrassment, the wine runs out. Mary notices the couple's need and brings it to the attention of her son. Mary does not command Jesus to do anything; she simply informs him, "They have no more wine." Jesus' reply sounds harsh: *"Woman,* what concern is that to you and to me? My hour has not yet come." Mary *is* "woman." She is the "new Eve," the "mother of all the living" present at the "new creation." Her "offspring" is the victorious one who crushes the head of the evil one. Mary turns confidently to the servants. "Do whatever he tells you," she says. Her son does not disappoint her. The water used for purification rites is changed into an abundance of "new wine." All who taste of it see and believe!

Mary's example assures us that God hears our prayers. If we ask in accord with the divine will, it will be ours. In baptism, we are begotten of God. As God's children, the true and eternal God will satisfy all our needs. As God's servants, we will do whatever we are told.

To Consider

- Do I intercede for the needs of others?
- Do I ask Mary to intercede for me?
- How have I experienced "new wine" in my life?

To Pray

Pray Psalm 149: Lord, I praise you in the assembly of the faithful. You adorn the lowly with victory. You exult your people in glory.

Epiphany (ABC)

Mt 2:1-12
  Isa 60:1-6; Ps 72; Eph 3:2-3,5-6

*Where is the child who has been born king of the Jews? For
we observed his star at its rising, and have come to pay him
homage. — Mt 2:2*

To Note

The solemnity of Epiphany (also called "Twelfth Day")
is celebrated on January 6 in commemoration of Christ's
glory revealed to the Gentiles in the persons of the Magi.
The Greek word *epiphaneia* means "manifestation," an
appearance of the divine. In the Eastern Church, the feast
(celebrated from the fourth century) includes the manifes-
tations of Christ at his baptism in the Jordan and the
miracle of the wedding feast of Cana. John's Gospel sees
the whole of Christ's life as an epiphany of the Messiah
and Son of God. Where the solemnity is not observed as a
holy day of obligation on January 6, the feast is transferred
to the Sunday between January 2 and 8.

To Understand

God's path to faith and peace was forgotten. In our darkness, it seemed impossible to find. The prophet tells us to
raise our eyes. The radiant light of God's glory appears
amidst the thick clouds that obscure our sight. All people
can walk by God's light. Our sons and daughters, held
captive to unbelief, violence, and addictions, return before
our eyes. Our hearts overflow for joy at the sight of this
great gift made manifest in Christ Jesus. We join in songs
of praise to Christ our light. He is our king who governs
the people with justice and the afflicted ones with judg-

ment. He rules from sea to sea, to the ends of the earth. Through him, peace and justice flower and spread forth their aroma everywhere.

"Where is this great king?" we ask in times of doubt and despair. We scan the heavens, desperately searching for a sign. Only those with eyes of faith can see the light from above; it goes before us to show the way. "Go and report your findings to me," say the Herods of this world, who want to destroy hope and faith. When we journey with the wise ones, what we discover is not a palace with a king on the throne surrounded by royal attendants. What we see is a simple house with a mother and her child. When we enter, we are in the household of faith. Our eyes are opened and we prostrate ourselves before the mystery revealed to us. We bring the finest treasures we can offer: gifts of gold, the splendor of faith and truth; gifts of frankincense, a fragrant offering of pure worship; gifts of myrrh, the sacrifice of suffering and death. When we present this great wealth, we rise anew to discover that we cannot return by the same road we have traveled before. We must follow a different path. It is Christ who reveals the way.

To Consider

- In what ways has Christ been revealed to me?
- What gifts do I offer in return?
- Do these gifts manifest Christ's reign of peace and justice on earth?

To Pray

Pray Psalm 73: Lord Jesus Christ, you are king of all the earth. May all peoples pay you homage and serve you with truth and love.

Baptism of the Lord (A)

Mt 3:13-17
    Isa 42:1-4,6-7; Ps 29; Acts 10:34-38

This is my Son, the Beloved, with whom I am well pleased.
— Mt 3:17

To Note

The Baptism of Jesus closes the Christmas season with another epiphany, or revelation, of Jesus. Jesus is directed by the Spirit from the time of his conception in his mother's womb to his sending the Spirit at Pentecost. Rebirth and life in the Spirit are distinguishing characteristics of Christian baptism. Baptism is a type of birth into the Christian community that makes one a daughter or son of God and "another Christ." Through the Spirit, the baptized woman or man "puts on" Christ (Rom 13:14). Clothed in Christ, as in a baptismal garment, Christians manifest him to the world.

To Understand

The servant of God makes his appearance: "Here is my servant, my chosen one with whom I am well pleased." The servant of the Lord brings forth justice; he knows his people are hurt and wounded, fragile as a blade of grass, frail as the smoldering wick of a candle. They are bent over, only a breath away from death. God's servant grasps us by the hand, forming and reforming us. We who are blind become a light to the nations. We who are imprisoned emerge from our private dungeons to live in freedom.

John and Jesus know what it is like to be God's servants. Jesus doesn't stand apart from the crowds. He makes his appearance among all who come to be baptized by John. The baptizer is overcome. Why does Jesus need baptism? Certainly he is sinless and has no need for conversion, the very purpose of John's baptism. "I should be baptized by you, yet you come to me," the servant protests to the master. Jesus implores, "Give in, John." Just as Jesus relinquishes his divine status, he urges John to let go of his preconceived notions. Jesus feels a oneness with his people and a compassion for their failures. He doesn't stand at the edge of the river telling how we mess things up or demanding that we be washed clean of our sins before he has anything to do with us. He invites us to step into the water with him. Jesus, the "beloved Son," submerges himself with his sinful brothers and sisters. By submitting to baptism, Jesus stands in solidarity with us all. We emerge from the waters recreated in his wonderful light.

To Consider

Prayerfully renew your own baptismal vows:

- Do I reject sin so that I might live in freedom with all God's children?
- Do I reject the glamor of evil and refuse to be mastered by sin?
- Do I believe in the Father, Son, and Spirit, the holy catholic church, the communion of saints, the forgiveness of sins, the resurrection of the body, and life everlasting?

To Pray

Pray Psalm 29: Lord Jesus Christ, we come in the holy attire of our baptism to give you glory and praise. With all people of peace, we proclaim you as Lord and king forever.

Baptism of the Lord (B)

Mk 1:7-11
  Isa 42:1-4,6-7; Ps 29; Acts 10:34-38

And just as he was coming up out of the water, he saw the heavens torn apart and the Spirit descending like a dove on him. — Mk 1:10

To Note

Matthew and Luke begin their Gospels with the nativity, the appearance of Jesus as Messiah and Son of God. Mark begins his Gospel with John the Baptist proclaiming the manifestation (epiphany) of Jesus in words and deeds. John heralds Jesus as one who is "mightier," who baptizes with the transforming power of the Holy Spirit. When John baptizes Jesus in the Jordan River, the heavens are "torn open," a manifestation of divine power that renews and restores God's people. At the cross, the veil in the temple is "torn" in two (Mk 15:38), a sign of the completion of Jesus' redeeming work. Today's feast marks the end of the Christmas season.

To Understand

God speaks and the heavens open; the chosen one is revealed. Just when we think we have things figured out, God turns our notions upside down. Our delusions and misconceptions are demolished. We must pick up the pieces and try to discover new aspects of God's revealed truth. God's anointed is not a powerful king or military leader. The one who pleases God is a servant of all, announcing peace and justice to everyone imprisoned by doubt and fear. Those who are blind see God's wisdom in a new light.

God speaks and Peter's eyes are opened. Peter thought he knew what God wanted. He believed that baptism was only for the "chosen" ones, the good and holy people who deserve God's mercy. Those "unclean" people didn't fit the picture. God has to reveal to Peter how blind he is. The heavens open and a voice is heard. "What God has made clean, you are not to call profane." God has no favorites. Whether one is rich or poor, strong or weak is unimportant to God. All that matters is that one strives to act with faith and moral decency.

God speaks and John sees Jesus as he really is, one mighty yet humble. Jesus, God's Son, becomes human like us—in all things but sin. Yet Jesus willingly unites himself to sinful humanity. In baptism, we become one with Christ. The mystery is incomprehensible to us. How can we dwell in Christ? What baffles us even more is how the trinity dwells in mere mortals. No church, no tabernacle, no monstrance nor chalice is as suitable a dwelling place for God as the human soul. The concept shatters our self-righteous arrogance. Our cold and prideful hearts are broken open by the love of God.

To Consider

- Reflect on what it means to dwell in Christ through baptism. Does this affect how you relate to others?
- Ponder the mystery of the Triune God dwelling in you as you prayerfully make the sign of the cross.

To Pray

Pray Psalm 29: Father, Son, and Spirit, your voice roars above the tumult, thunders over voices of doubt and despair. You have blessed your people with peace.

Baptism of the Lord (C)

Lk 3:15-16,21-22
    Isa 42:1-4,6-7; Ps 29; Acts 10:34-38

I baptize you with water; but one who is more powerful than I is coming....He will baptize you with the Holy Spirit and fire. — Lk 3:16

To Note

The U.S. Bishops state that the appropriate time and place to baptize adults and children older than six years is at the Easter vigil on Holy Saturday. Vatican Council II restored the ancient order of the catechumenate, incorporating steps and stages for those preparing for the rites of Christian initiation (*Rite of Christian Initiation of Adults* [RCIA]). Initiation into the Christian community is followed by a period of *mystagogy*, a time of exploration and formation to unfold the fullness of the sacrament(s) received. Where the process is vibrant, the RCIA can be a catechizing tool and a center for renewal for the entire parish community.

To Understand

The people are full of anticipation. They stand on tip-toes as they await God's chosen one. They wonder, "Could John be the Messiah of God?" John protests. How can they be so blind to God's revelation? Why are they imprisoned in darkness? When will they see the truth? "I baptize you in water," John explains, "but there is one to come who is mightier." John knows he is only a lowly servant. The one God sends will not simply perform a ritual signifying a need to repent. God's anointed one will baptize the people in the Holy Spirit and in fire. All their impurities will be burned away like dross, leaving them pure and sinless.

126

Those who come to John for baptism do not recognize that Jesus is the one sent by God. They are surprised when a dove descends from the heavens and they hear a voice declare, "You are my beloved. On you my favor rests." They are unsure if the voice is meant for them or for the one who stands shoulder to shoulder with them in the chilly waters, gently warming them with the fire of his love.

Peter slowly comes to understand how little he has understood. He has been suspicious and hostile toward those who were not of his race and beliefs. He was certain that his mission was only to his own, not to "those people." Peter is graphically shown that God has no favorites. Any upright person of faith is acceptable to God. This is the message of peace that Jesus proclaimed from the time of his baptism. Jesus invites us to share his work in the same way he shares our baptism. Jesus, anointed by the power of the Holy Spirit, went about doing good works and healing all those in the grip of evil. This is the good news that we must proclaim. When we do, we will hear God's voice declaring, "You are my beloved sons and daughters. In you I am well pleased."

To Consider

- Have I grown in my understanding of God's revelation in Scripture and the church during this Advent and Christmas season?
- Am I a sign of Christ's presence today?

To Pray

Pray Psalm 29: Lord Jesus Christ, we hear your voice over the waters of baptism, blessing and uniting all your brothers and sisters with love, peace, and harmony.

Index of Lectionary References

Genesis

3:9-15,20. 76
49:2,8-10. 60

Numbers

6:22-27 106
24:2-7,15-17 44

Judges

13:2-7,24-25 64

1 Samuel

1:24-28 70
2:1,4-8
(used as psalm) 70

2 Samuel

7:1-5,8-11,16 . . . . . . 56, 74

Psalms

1 34
23 12
24 . . . . 54, 66
25 . . . . 6, 44, 72
27 16
29 . . . . 122, 124, 126
30 50
31 88
33 68
34 46
67 . . . . 52, 106

71. 64
72. . . . . . 10, 20, 60, 62, 120
80. . . . . 4, 36, 58
85. . . . . 22, 26, 48
89. . . . . 56, 74, 80
96. . . . . . . 28, 82, 94, 96, 98
97. . . . . 84, 90
98. . . . . 76, 86, 108, 110, 112
100. 114
103. 30
118. 14
122. . . . . 2, 8
124. 92
126. 24
128. . . . . 100, 102, 104
145. 32
146. 38
147. . . . . 18, 116
149. 118

Song of Solomon

2:8-14 68

Isaiah

2:1-5 . . . . 2, 8
4:2-6 8
7:10-14 . . . . 54, 66
9:1-6 82
11:1-10 . . . . 10, 20
12. 42
25:6-10 12

129

Isaiah (*continued*)

26:1-6	14
29:17-24	16
30:19-21,23-26	18
35:1-6,10	38
35:1-10	26
40:1-5,9-11	22
40:1-11	28
40:25-31	30
41:13-20	32
42:1-4,6-7	122, 124, 126
45:6-8,18,21-25	48
48:17-19	34
52:7-10	86
54:1-10	50
56:1-3,6-8	52
60:1-6	120
61:1-2,10-11	40
62:1-5	80
62:11-12	84
63:16-17,19, 64:2-7	4

Jeremiah

23:5-8	62
33:14-16	6

Micah

5:1-4	58

Zephaniah

3:1-2,9-13	46
3:14-18	42, 68

Malachi

3:1-4,23-24	72

Sirach

3:2-6,12-14	100, 102, 104
48:1-4,9-11	36

Baruch

5:1-9	24

Matthew

1:1-17	60
1:1-25	80
1:18-24	54, 62
2:1-12	120
2:13-15,19-23	100
2:13-18	92
3:1-12	20
3:13-17	122
7:21,24-27	14
8:5-11	8
9:27-31	16
9:35-10:1,6-8	18
10:17-22	88
11:2-11	38
11:11-15	32
11:16-19	34
11:28-30	30
15:29-37	12
17:10-13	36
18:12-14	28
21:23-27	44